Sports Law in Singapore

Sports Law in Singapore

Hamidul Haq
Michelle Lee Sze Min

This book was originally published as a monograph in the International Encyclopaedia of Laws/Sports Law.

Founding Editor: Roger Blanpain
General Editor: Frank Hendrickx
Volume Editor: Michele Colucci

Wolters Kluwer

Published by:
Kluwer Law International B.V.
PO Box 316
2400 AH Alphen aan den Rijn
The Netherlands
E-mail: lrs-sales@wolterskluwer.com
Website: www.wolterskluwer.com/en/solutions/kluwerlawinternational

Sold and distributed by:
Wolters Kluwer Legal & Regulatory U.S.
920 Links Avenue
Landisville, PA 17538
United States of America
E-mail: customer.service@wolterskluwer.com

ISBN 978-94-035-2388-0

e-Book: ISBN 978-94-035-2398-9
web-PDF: ISBN 978-94-035-2408-5

The Authors

Hamidul Haq has been a partner with Rajah & Tann Singapore LLP since 2006. He holds a Bachelor of Laws (Hons) from the National University of Singapore and a Master's degree in Corporate and Commercial Law from University College London.

Mr Haq started his career at the Criminal Justice Division, Attorney-General's Chambers, rising to Deputy Senior State Counsel. He subsequently acted as Head Legal for the Commercial Affairs Department of the Singapore Police Force for eight years, before joining Rajah & Tann Singapore LLP.

In his position as Head of the White Collar Crime Division, Mr Haq led the team that successfully challenged the detention under the Criminal Law (Temporary Provisions) Act (Cap 67) of a person allegedly involved in an international match-fixing ring, achieving victory before Singapore's Court of Appeal (*Tan Seet Eng v. Attorney-General and Another Matter* [2016] 1 SLR 779). Mr Haq has acted in other match-fixing cases and gambling cases and has provided advice in local sports-related investigations. Mr Haq also leads the firm's Fraud, Asset Recovery and Investigations division.

Mr Haq holds a number of appointments in the sports sector, including as the sole Prosecutor for Anti-Doping Singapore, Prosecutor for the Southeast Asia Regional Anti-Doping Organization, Member of the Singapore Hockey Federation Disciplinary Committee, Member of the Football Association of Singapore Ethics Committee and Member of the Singapore Silat Federation Disciplinary Committee.

Michelle Lee Sze Min is a partner with Rajah & Tann Singapore LLP. She holds a Bachelor of Laws and a Master's with a specialisation in Commercial Law from King's College London.

Ms Lee is a litigator with significant experience in defending clients in criminal and extradition matters. She has also handled civil court matters concerning issues such as trusts and civil harassment. Her advisory experience is broad, dealing with issues relating to anti-corruption, cheating, drugs, market manipulation, insider trading, seizure and confiscation orders, reporting obligations, food licensing, employment and workplace health and safety. Ms Lee has also been involved in conducting investigations for multinational entities.

The Authors

Table of Contents

Table of Contents

Table of Contents

List of Abbreviations

ACW	Active Citizens Worldwide
AD Policy	Anti-doping Policy of Singapore
AD Rules	ADS Anti-doping Rules
ADR Sports	Framework for Alternative Dispute Resolution for Sports
ADS	Anti-doping Singapore
Advisory Guidelines	Advisory Guidelines on Key Concepts in the PDPA (revised on 16 May 2022)
CDSA	Corruption, Drug Trafficking and Other Serious Crimes (Confiscation of Benefits) Act 1992
Charities Code	Code of Governance for Charities and Institutions of a Public Character
CLTPA	Criminal Law (Temporary Provisions) Act 1955
Conduct Code	Code of Practice for Market Conduct in the Provision of Media Services
Copyright Act	Copyright Act (Cap 63)
CPC	Criminal Procedure Code 2010
CPF	Central Provident Fund
CPFTA	Consumer Protection (Fair Trading) Act 2003
CPIB	Corrupt Practices Investigation Bureau
CYPAct	Children and Young Persons Act 1993
EFMA	Employment of Foreign Manpower Act 1990
FAS	Football Association of Singapore
FCTC	World Health Organisation Framework Convention on Tobacco Control
FIA	Fédération Internationale de l'Automobile
FIDE	World Chess Federation
FSTS	Foreign Sports Talent Scheme
GCA	Gambling Control Act 2022
GRA	Gambling Regulatory Authority

List of Abbreviations

GRA Act	Gambling Regulatory Authority of Singapore Act 2022
IMDA	Info-communications Media Development Authority
IMDAA	Info-communications Media Development Authority Act 2016
INTERPOL	International Criminal Police Organization
IOC	International Olympic Committee
IPOS	Intellectual Property Office of Singapore
IRAS	Inland Revenue Authority of Singapore
MCCY	Ministry of Culture, Community and Youth
MDAct	Misuse of Drugs Act
MediaCorp	MediaCorp Singapore
NROC	National Registry of Coaches
NS	National Service
NSA	National Sports Association
NSPS	National Sports Participation Survey
OCA	Organised Crime Act 2015
PCA	Prevention of Corruption Act 1960
PDPA	Personal Data Protection Act 2012
Penal Code	Penal Code 1871
POHA	Protection from Harassment Act 2014
PP v. Kannan	*Kannan s/o Kunjiraman and Another v. Public Prosecutor* [1995] 3 SLR(R) 294
RADO	Regional Anti-doping Organization
RSTP	Regulations on the Status and Transfer of Players
SBBF	Singapore Bodybuilding Federation
SEARADO	Southeast Asia Regional Anti-doping Organization
Singapore Pools	Singapore Pools (Private) Limited
Singtel	Singapore Telecommunications Limited
SNOC	Singapore National Olympic Council
Societies Code	Code of Governance for Registered Societies
Spandeck	*Spandeck Engineering (S) Pte Ltd v. Defence Science & Technology Agency* [2007] 4 SLR(R) 100
spexBusiness	Sports Excellence Business Network
spexCarding	Sports Excellence Carding System
spexCareer	Sports Excellence Career Scheme
spexEducation	Sports Excellence Education Scheme
spexPotential	Sports Excellence Potential programme
spexScholarship	Sports Excellence Scholarship
SportSG	Sport Singapore
SSC	Singapore Sports Council

SSI	Singapore Sports Institute
StarHub	StarHub Ltd
STBC	Singapore Tenpin Bowling Congress
STR	Suspicious Transaction Report
STTA	Singapore Table Tennis Association
The Law of Torts	Gary Chan Kok Yew, *The Law of Torts in Singapore* (2nd ed., Academy Publishing, 2016)
TMA	Trade Marks Act 1998
Tobacco Act	Tobacco (Control of Advertisements and Sale) Act 1993
Tote Board	Singapore Totalisator Board
ULIS	United Lotteries for Integrity in Sports
WAD Code	World Anti-doping Code
WADA	World Anti-doping Agency

List of Abbreviations

General Introduction

§1. State of Sports Law in Singapore

1. Singapore is a relatively young nation, having celebrated its 50th birthday in 2015. During the early years of independence, the foremost concerns for the Government were national survival and nation-building. Problems faced at the time include racial tension, housing shortage, unemployment and overpopulation. The Government developed a number of economic and social policies to target these problems, such as industrialisation, the rapid and large-scale construction of public housing, a focus on education to grow the education infrastructure, promoting family planning and campaigns to promote civic conscientiousness. A culture of meritocracy was also promoted in order to equalise opportunities. Rewards are allocated based on a person's merits or abilities and not by discriminating factors such as race or religion.

2. Less focus was given to the development of sports. However, in recent years, Singapore has placed more emphasis on promoting sports culture and developing athletes who can compete at an international level. The Government has increased funding for sports and ramped up the quality and quantity of sports facilities, especially with the official opening of the Singapore Sports Hub in 2015. The Singapore Sports Hub is located on a 35-hectare site and incorporates the National Stadium. It contains several facilities, such as an aquatic centre, water sports centre, retail mall, skate park, sports library, museum and restaurants.

3. Several international sports events have been hosted in Singapore over the past few years. In the past two decades, Singapore has played host to several high-profile events, including the Fédération Internationale de l'Automobile (hereinafter 'FIA') Formula One Singapore Grand Prix, the World Rugby Singapore Sevens and the Women's Tennis Association Finals. It also hosted the Summer Youth Olympic Games in 2010 and matches for the 2018 International Champions Cup.

4. In terms of legislation, there is no specific sports-related legislation (other than the administrative legislation that governs the national sports council of Singapore).[1] Instead, legislation relied upon to resolve sports-related issues relates to other areas of law, such as intellectual property law, criminal law, contract law,

1. Namely, the Singapore Sports Council Act 1973.

employment law and media law. A cause of action founded in tort (such as tort of negligence or tort of passing off) may also occur. Currently, there are few lawyers in Singapore who specialise in sports law on a full-time basis.

§2. Statistics

5. Since 1987, the statutory board Sport Singapore (formerly known as the Singapore Sports Council) (hereinafter 'SportSG') has provided an indicator of local sports culture through the National Sports Participation Survey (hereinafter 'NSPS'), which is a Singapore-wide study conducted among Singapore citizens and permanent residents who are at least 13 years old.[2] Until 2015, the survey was carried out every five years. From 2015, the NSPS was converted to an annual survey with monthly interviews.[3] Between 2018 and 2022, the percentage of those who participate in sports or exercise increased from 66% to 74%.[4]

6. Another source of information was the global network Active Citizens Worldwide (hereinafter 'ACW'), which was founded by London, Auckland and Singapore. ACW used data to provide policymakers in cities across the world with sufficient knowledge, insights and ideas to transform the physical activity profiles of their cities.[5] ACW's 2018 Annual Report noted that the top five sports in Singapore are walking, jogging, gym, football and bicycle touring.[6] Three-quarters of physical activity takes place in public facilities.[7] 'Lack of time because of work/school' was the most popular reason for not engaging in physical activity;[8] this was reflected in a drop of 30% in physical activity from the 13–15 to 25–34 age groups.[9] Sports provided active residents in Singapore with opportunities for inter-group contact, with regular participation in sports contributing 119 hours of positive social contact each year, comprising sixty-two hours with individuals of a different race, forty-three hours with individuals of a different age group and seven hours with individuals with disability.[10]

---

2. SportSG, *Sports Participation in Singapore*, https://www.sportsingapore.gov.sg/about-us/sports-particpation-in-singapore (accessed 18 Jan. 2019).
3. SportSG, *Sports Participation in Singapore*, https://www.sportsingapore.gov.sg/support-resources/sports-participation-in-singapore/ (accessed 22 Nov. 2023).
4. SportSG, *National Sport Participation Survey 2018–2022*, https://6212555.fs1.hubspotusercontent-na1.net/hubfs/6212555/ActiveSG-SportDexSG/files/2023%20Sports%20SG%20-%20National%20Sport%20Participation%20Survey%20Brochure_SinglePage%20(22.06.2023)%20Final.pdf (accessed 22 Nov. 2023).
5. Active Citizens Worldwide, *About ACW*, https://web.archive.org/web/20190415000000*/http://activecitizens.world/about-acw/ (accessed 18 Jan. 2019).
6. ACW 2018 Annual Report, p. 30 (viewable at http://activecitizens.world/media/1327/acw-2018-annual-report-lo-res.pdf).
7. ACW 2018 Annual Report, p. 33.
8. *Ibid.*, p. 31.
9. *Ibid.*, pp. 41 and 42.
10. *Ibid.*, p. 61.

§3. Vision 2030

7. Vision 2030 is a blueprint drawn up in 2012 to answer the question, 'How can Sport best serve Singapore to serve the best interests of Singapore in developing healthy resilient people and strong united communities?'[11] SportSG received several hundred unique ideas, which were then categorised and crystallised into twenty recommendations that were implemented as the pillars of Vision 2030.[12] Four themes emerged, namely:

(1) Future Ready Through Sports.
(2) Sports Without Boundaries.
(3) Sports as a National Language.
(4) Organising for Success.

8. Under the theme 'Future Ready Through Sports', a Sports Pathways Committee was set up to collaborate in the development of sports pathways for youth.[13] The Super Sports Club is a recommendation that aims to promote a strong sports culture by making over existing sports facilities and setting up sports centres that offer programmes and activities for people of differing needs, skills and fitness levels.[14]

9. For the theme 'Sport Without Boundaries', the aim is to make sports accessible, affordable and appropriate for all.[15] This is facilitated through the Sports Facilities Master Plan, which will be implemented through the construction of new sports facilities and rejuvenation of existing facilities with innovative features.[16]

10. 'Sport as a National Language' involves bringing people of different cultural and ethnic groups together and building a bridge that links the different communities, whether by engaging in sports together or by supporting national athletes.[17]

11. 'Organising for Success' emphasises the need for all key agencies, including private sector organisations, to coordinate their efforts in order to bring about Vision 2030.

---

11. Vision 2030 Steering Committee Report 2012, p. 4, viewable at https://www.mccy.gov.sg/about-us/news-and-resources/statistics/2019/jan/-/media/0E5F60864A604FE7B4C007DEF6FB7FA8.ashx (accessed 22 Nov. 2023).
12. SportSG, *Vision 2030*, https://www.sportsingapore.gov.sg/about-us/vision-2030/ (accessed 22 Nov. 2023).
13. *Singapore Sports Guide 2013/2014* (Marshall Cavendish 8th ed. 2013), p. 13.
14. SportSG, *Super Sports Club*, https://www.sportsingapore.gov.sg/About-Us/Vision-2030/Super-Sports-Club (accessed 18 Jan. 2019).
15. *Singapore Sports Guide 2013/2014* (Marshall Cavendish 8th ed. 2013), p. 13.
16. Ministry of Culture, Community and Youth, *Sports Facilities Master Plan*, https://www.mccy.gov.sg/sector/initiatives/sports-facilities-master-plan (accessed 18 Jan. 2019).
17. *Singapore Sports Guide 2013/2014* (Marshall Cavendish 8th ed. 2013), pp. 13 and 14.

§4. Institutions

12. Singapore's sports administrative infrastructure comprises the following governmental entities: the Ministry of Culture, Community and Youth (MCCY); SportSG; the Singapore National Olympic Council (SNOC); and the individual National Sports Associations (NSAs). Below the level of the NSAs are the clubs and organisations that participate in the sports and which are members or affiliates of the respective NSAs.

13. Anti-Doping Singapore (hereinafter 'ADS') was established in 2010 as Singapore's national anti-doping organisation. ADS is a division within SportSG. As the country's national anti-doping organisation, ADS is responsible for planning, coordinating and implementing an effective doping control programme.

Part I. Organisation of Sports

Chapter 1. Sports Governance

§1. Governmental Institutions and Bodies

I. Ministry of Culture, Community and Youth

14. The MCCY is the Government ministry that 'seeks to inspire Singaporeans through the arts and sports, strengthen community bonds, and promote volunteerism and philanthropy'.[18] In relation to sports, the MCCY's functions are as follows:[19]

- Encouraging community participation and engagement in sports.
- Supporting the sports aspirations of our people, sports excellence and education.
- Developing Singapore's sports industry and infrastructure for a vibrant sports culture and a better quality of life.

II. Sport Singapore

15. SportSG (formerly known as the Singapore Sports Council) is a statutory board of the Government and was established under the Singapore Sports Council Act 1973. SportSG reports to MCCY.

16. SportSG's core purpose is 'to inspire the Singapore spirit and transform Singapore through sport'.[20] Its functions include planning and promoting competitive and recreational sports in Singapore, coordinating sports activities in Singapore, fostering research and study in sports and physical education and establishing sports facilities and clubs for the promotion of sports.[21]

17. SportSG manages sports building in Singapore by working with the individual NSAs for each sport, as well as with public and private sector partners. In

18. Ministry of Culture, Community and Youth, *About Us*, https://www.mccy.gov.sg/About-us.aspx (accessed 24 Jul. 2018).
19. *Ibid.*
20. SportSG, *2014/2015: Celebrating an Extraordinary Year*, https://www.sportsingapore.gov.sg/files/Media%20Centre/Annual%20Reports/14_15.pdf, p. 4 (accessed 22 Nov. 2023).
21. Singapore Sports Council Act 1973, s. 8.

2011, SportSG launched the Singapore Sports Institute (hereinafter 'SSI') with the objective of supporting and nurturing Singapore's athletes through science and technology.[22] The SSI provides support through schemes such as the Sports Excellence Scholarship (spexScholarship),[23] Sports Excellence Career Scheme[24] (spexCareer) and Sports Excellence Education Scheme (spexEducation).[25] It also provides support in the areas of training, competition, coaching, sports medicine and sports science.[26]

18. In terms of coaching, SportSG offers theoretical and practical coach development programmes to guide coaches on how to nurture athletes.[27] SportSG also manages the National Registry of Coaches (hereinafter 'NROC'). All coaches in the NROC are certified under the Singapore Coach Excellence Programme in their respective sports. This programme seeks to provide aspiring coaches with the knowledge and skills of 'how to coach' and to guide them to understand 'why you coach' through the introduction of values education and principles in sports within the local ecosystem.[28]

19. Furthermore, all coaches in the NROC must hold Standard First Aid certification. They are committed to abide by the Coach's Code of Ethics and meet the requirements for the Continuing Coach Education Programme operated by the SSI.[29] The NROC thus gives recognition to qualified coaches. The database of NROC coaches is publicly available[30] and may be accessed by any member of the public looking for a coach.

20. Under the Coach's Code of Ethics, coaches are bound to abide by three principles: (1) respect for individuals, (2) responsible coaching and (3) integrity in

22. SportSG (11 Jul. 2013), *Opening Remarks By Mr Richard Seow, Chairman, Singapore Sports Council, at the Launch of the 2013 Singapore Sports Institute Annual Symposium*, https://www.sportsingapore.gov.sg/newsroom/speeches/2013/7/opening-remarks-by-mr-richard-seow-at-the-launch-of-the-2013-ssi-annual-symposium (accessed 24 Jul. 2018).
23. SportSG, *High Performance Planning*, https://www.sportsingapore.gov.sg/athletes-coaches/singapore-sports-institute/high-performance-sports/high-performance-planning (accessed 24 Jul. 2018).
24. SportSG, *spexBusiness*, https://www.sportsingapore.gov.sg/athletes-coaches/singapore-sports-institute/athlete-services-and-development/spexbusiness (accessed 24 Jul. 2018).
25. SportSG, *spexEducation*, https://www.sportsingapore.gov.sg/athletes-coaches/singapore-sports-institute/athlete-services-and-development/spexeducation (accessed 24 Jul. 2018).
26. SportSG, *Singapore Sport Institute*, https://www.sportsingapore.gov.sg/athletes-coaches/singapore-sports-institute (accessed 24 Jul. 2018).
27. SportSG, *Coaches' Corner*, https://www.sportsingapore.gov.sg/athletes-coaches/coaches-corner (accessed 24 Jul. 2018).
28. SportSG, *SG-Coach Level 1 Theory Programme*, https://www.sportsingapore.gov.sg/Athletes-Coaches/Coaches-Corner/Singapore-Coach-Excellence-Programme-SG-Coach/SG-Coach-Level-1-Theory-Programme (accessed 18 Jan. 2019).
29. SportSG, *National Registry of Coaches (NROC)*, https://www.sportsingapore.gov.sg/athletes-coaches/coaches-corner/national-registry-of-coaches (accessed 24 Jul. 2018).
30. The database may be accessed via https://www.activesgcircle.gov.sg/nrep/find-a-coach (accessed 22 Nov. 2023).

actions.[31] In particular, the coach must be mindful that (a) each individual possesses an intrinsic value and worth, (b) risks to athletes are to be minimised and benefits to their holistic development are to be maximised and (c) the coach is expected to be honest, principled and honourable.[32]

21. In the event that the NSA receives any complaint or information relating to a potential breach of the Coach's Code of Ethics, the NSA shall keep SportSG updated as soon as reasonably possible.[33] Investigations must be carried out in accordance with the NSA's disciplinary by-laws and/or as documented in the NSA's governing instruments.[34] Disciplinary actions that can be meted out include being required to issue an apology, being issued with a warning letter or having one's NROC membership suspended or terminated.[35]

22. In terms of sports safety, SportSG and fourteen other organisations and medical institutions together comprise the Sports Safety Working Committee. The Working Committee aims to promote sports safety through a multi-year, multi-prong Sports Safety Plan.[36] It is responsible for looking into the implementation of recommendations by the Sports Safety Committee. These recommendations are set out in the Sports Safety Committee Report (latest edition released in 2019[37]) and address multiple areas such as carrying out pre-participation screening, water safety, prevention of sudden cardiac arrest or sudden cardiac death, prevention of heat injury, and event medical support and coverage.

§2. National Olympic Committee and Sports Associations

I. Singapore National Olympic Council

23. The SNOC (formerly known as the Singapore Olympic and Sports Council) is a non-profit organisation that was formed in 1947, before Singapore's achievement of independence in 1965. The SNOC coordinates the selection of athletes to represent Singapore at major international sports events such as the Olympics, the Asian Games, the Commonwealth Games and the Southeast Asian Games.

24. The aims of the SNOC are set out in its Constitution. They include the promotion of general interest for sports in Singapore, encouraging the development of

31. Coach's Code of Ethics (accessible at https://6212555.fs1.hubspotusercontent-na1.net/hubfs/6212555/CID_NROC%20Handbook%20(20231023).pdf, pp. 22–24), Art. 3.
32. Coach's Code of Ethics, Arts 4–6.
33. Breach of Coach's Code of Ethics: Disciplinary Guidelines (accessible at https://6212555.fs1.hubspotusercontent-na1.net/hubfs/6212555/CID_NROC%20Handbook%20(20231023).pdf, pp. 24–25), Art. 4.3.
34. Breach of Coach's Code of Ethics: Disciplinary Guidelines, Art. 5.2.
35. *Ibid.*, Art. 5.5.
36. SportSG, *Sports Safety*, https://www.sportsingapore.gov.sg/sports-education/sports-safety/introduction/ (accessed 22 Nov. 2023).
37. Accessible at https://www.sportsingapore.gov.sg/files/Sport%20Education/Sport%20Safety/2019_Sports_Safety_Committee_Report_30Oct19(4).pdf (accessed 22 Nov. 2023).

sports for all, developing and protecting the Olympic Movement in Singapore, ensuring the observance of the Olympic Charter in Singapore and joining the fight against doping by ensuring the observance of the World Anti-Doping Code (WAD Code).[38]

25. Training programmes for coaches, officials and athletes are funded annually through the Olympic Solidarity programme, which is sponsored by the International Olympic Committee (hereinafter 'IOC'). The SNOC evaluates and approves proposals for technical courses that raise the skills of local coaches and officials.

26. The SNOC also partners with third parties for funding and sponsorship. For example, in 2013, the NTUC Fairprice Foundation provided sports scholarships to medallists who performed well at youth games.[39] In 2015, the international fitness centre brand Fitness First signed a three-year deal to sponsor SGD 1.3 million in international membership to support athlete development of Team Singapore.[40] In July 2017 and again in August 2023, the telecommunications company Singapore Telecommunications Limited (hereinafter 'Singtel') and SNOC renewed their partnership for five-year periods. Under the terms of the partnership, Singtel funds the training of Team Singapore athletes competing in various sports events, including the 2017 SEA Games, the Gold Coast 2018 Commonwealth Games and the 2020 Tokyo Olympics. The company also provides support through its mobile plans for Team Singapore.[41]

27. As an incentive to athletes, the SNOC operates a scheme known as the Major Games Award Programme (formerly the Multi-Million Dollar Award Programme), which provides a cash payout to athletes who win medals at the Olympic, Asian, Commonwealth and Southeast Asian Games. The largest award is SGD 1 million, given to an athlete who wins an individual gold medal at the Olympic Games. The award is taxable, and the athlete is required to plough back at least 20% of the award to his/her NSA for future training and development.[42]

---

38. Constitution of the Singapore National Olympic Council, Art. 2.1.1.
39. Singapore National Olympic Council (4 Dec. 2013), *NTUC FairPrice Foundation Presents Sports Scholarships to Asian Youth Games Medallists*, http://www.singaporeolympics.com/ntuc-fairprice-foundation-presents-sports-scholarships-to-asian-youth-games-medallists/ (accessed 24 Jul. 2018).
40. Fitness First Singapore (16 Nov. 2015), *Fitness First Cements 3-Year Sponsorship with Team Singapore*, https://www.fitnessfirst.com.sg/press-room/news/official-fitness-partner-of-singapore-national-olympic-council/ (accessed 24 Jul. 2018).
41. Singtel (22 Jul. 2017), *Singtel Renews Partnership with Singapore National Olympic Council to Support Team Singapore Athletes*, https://www.singtel.com/about-us/media-centre/news-releases/-singtel-renews-partnership-with-singapore-national-olympic-council-to-suport (accessed 22 Nov. 2023), and Singtel (5 Aug. 2023), *Singtel and Singapore National Olympic Council renew longstanding partnership*, https://www.singtel.com/about-us/media-centre/news-releases/-singtel-and-singapore-national-olympic-council-renew-longstandi (accessed 22 Nov. 2023).
42. *Singapore National Olympic Council Major Games Award Programme 2022 to 2024,* (accessible at https://www.singaporeolympics.com/wp-content/uploads/2022/07/SNOC-MAP-2022-2024.pdf), Art. 5.

28. Article 8.1.1 of the SNOC's Constitution grants the SNOC's Executive Committee the power to enquire into any breach of the Constitution and any of the SNOC's by-laws or to appoint a subcommittee for that purpose. The offending NSA or athlete can be cautioned, expelled from the SNOC or dealt with in any manner thought fit by the Executive Committee. Any NSA or person against whom such a decision is made can file an appeal during an Extraordinary General Meeting of the SNOC,[43] or may appeal to the Court of Arbitration for Sports based in Lausanne, Switzerland.[44] The decision of the Court of Arbitration for Sports shall be final and binding on all parties.[45]

29. As an example of the SNOC's exercise of its Article 8.1.1 power, in August 2017, a marathoner was sent a formal and final warning by the SNOC for allegedly repeatedly breaching rules regarding the promotion of personal sponsors on social media. It was reported that the marathoner was warned that he would be expelled from Singapore's Southeast Asian Games team if he failed to comply.[46]

II. National Sports Associations

30. At the national level, each sport is typically governed by an NSA. For an organisation to be recognised by SportSG as an NSA of a particular sport, the organisation has to demonstrate that it enjoys the support and mandate of the sport's local fraternity and is in good financial health with varied sources of revenue, among other criteria.[47]

31. It is not unprecedented for an organisation to lose its status as an NSA. On 8 May 2019, World Taekwondo and the SNOC both suspended the Singapore Taekwondo Federation as an affiliate with immediate effect. It was reported that World Taekwondo had written to the SNOC in October 2018 expressing concern after the mass resignations of seven Singapore Taekwondo Federation management committee members and that SNOC had 'grave concerns in the governance and high-performance management of STF'.[48] The SNOC announced that it would work with SportSG to set up a major games preparation committee to manage the selection of national taekwondo athletes.[49] A new management committee was voted in on 26

43. SNOC Constitution, Art. 8.2.1(a).
44. *Ibid.*, Art. 8.2.2(a).
45. *Ibid.*, Art. 8.2.2(b).
46. Lin Fhoong, Low (14 Aug. 2017), *Marathoner Soh Given Last Warning for Breaching SNOC Rules*, Today, https://www.todayonline.com/sports/marathoner-soh-given-last-warning-breaching-snoc-rules (accessed 22 Feb. 2019).
47. Ms Grace Fu Hai Yien (8 May 2017), *Singapore Parliamentary Report vol. 94*, col. 29, available at https://sprs.parl.gov.sg/search/#/sprs3topic?reportid=written-answer-na-3531 (accessed 25 Feb. 2019).
48. Lin Fhoong, Low (8 May 2019), *Singapore Taekwondo Federation suspended by SNOC and world body*, Today, https://www.todayonline.com/singapore/singapore-taekwondo-federation-suspended-snoc-and-world-body (accessed 29 Mar. 2021).
49. *Ibid.*

September 2020.[50] The SNOC lifted STF's suspension with effect from 26 January 2023,[51] and World Taekwondo lifted STF's suspension on 28 May 2023.[52]

A. *Funding*

32. In order for an NSA to receive funding from SportSG, it must be registered both as a society under the Societies Act 1966 and as a charity under the Charities Act 1994. In addition, NSAs have to develop multi-year strategic plans for the respective sport, with key deliverables aligned with SportSG's objectives.[53] The plans, which include desired outcomes, can be discussed and agreed upon with SportSG. The plans can include areas such as youth and coaching development, and community outreach and participation.[54]

33. SportSG's grants to the NSAs help to support their organisation functions, outreach programmes, training facilities and High Performance Sports plans. The level of funding is assessed from year to year, taking into account factors such as whether the NSA has achieved the agreed key performance indicators, the NSA's capabilities in governance and execution and whether there is a sound plan for the development of the sport that is supported by the NSA's members.[55]

B. *Codes of Governance, Societies Act and Charities Act*

34. NSAs that are registered as societies are subject to the Code of Governance for Registered Societies (hereinafter 'Societies Code'), whereas NSAs that are registered as charities are subject to the Code of Governance for Charities and Institutions of a Public Character (hereinafter 'Charities Code'). Up to November 2007, NSAs were subject to the Code of Governance for National Sports Associations, but this has been since superseded by the Charities Code.

50. Sazali Abdul Aziz (17 Dec. 2020), *Governance, high performance the focus as S'pore Taekwondo Federation's new leaders work to lift suspension*, The Straits Times, https://www.straitstimes.com/sport/combat-sports/governance-high-performance-the-focus-as-spore-taekwondo-federations-new-leaders (accessed 29 Mar. 2021).
51. Singapore Taekwondo Federation (8 Mar. 2023), *Singapore National Olympic Council Lifted The Suspension Of Singapore Taekwondo Federation*, https://www.stf.sg/news/local-news/singapore-national-olympic-council-lifted-the-suspension-of-singapore-taekwondo-federation/ (accessed 22 Nov. 2023).
52. Singapore Taekwondo Federation (3 Jun. 2023), *Singapore Taekwondo Federation's Return to the Global Taekwondo Family*, https://www.stf.sg/news/local-news/singapore-taekwondo-federations-return-to-the-global-taekwondo-family/ (accessed 22 Nov. 2023).
53. Ms Grace Fu Hai Yien (8 May 2017), *Singapore Parliamentary Report vol. 94*, col. 29, available at https://sprs.parl.gov.sg/search/#/sprs3topic?reportid=written-answer-na-3531 (accessed 25 Feb. 2019).
54. Ms Grace Fu Hai Yien (1 Aug. 2017), *Singapore Parliamentary Report vol. 94*, col. 71, available at https://sprs.parl.gov.sg/search/#/sprs3topic?reportid=written-answer-na-3733 (accessed 25 Feb. 2019).
55. Ms Grace Fu Hai Yien (8 May 2017), *Singapore Parliamentary Report vol. 94*, col. 29, available at https://sprs.parl.gov.sg/search/#/sprs3topic?reportid=written-answer-na-3531 (accessed 25 Feb. 2019).

35. The Societies Code aims to enhance the governance of societies and to provide guidance to management committees as they carry out their duties and act in the interest of their members.[56]

36. Registered societies are also subject to statutory obligations under the Societies Act 1966. For example, if the Registrar of Societies requests information or documentation from the society, and if the society fails to comply with the whole or part of such order, then the persons who were served with the order (typically the society's officers) can be found guilty of an offence and liable on conviction to a fine.[57] Restrictions are also placed on persons who can act as officers of a society: a person who has been convicted of an offence involving the unlawful expenditure of the funds of the society while being a member of the society, or a person who has been declared by the Minister as being unfit to act as officer due to a criminal conviction, may not act as an officer.[58] In addition, under section 19 of the Act, if an officer or member of the society has unlawfully withheld any money of the society or wilfully applied such money to purposes other than those expressed or directed in the rules of the society and authorised by the Act, then the court can order that person to return the money to the trustees of the society. Failure to obey the court order amounts to an offence punishable by fine.

37. The Charities Code aims to (a) make charities more effective by sharing recommended practices, (b) provide guidance to board members and (c) boost public confidence in the charity sector.[59] The latter is important as members of the public donate and volunteer their services to charities.

38. The Charities Code operates on the principle of 'comply or explain' and is not mandatory. If the charity is not able to comply with certain guidelines, it has to explain the circumstances (e.g., because the charity is in the process of working towards compliance). Charities are also encouraged to review their governing instruments, by-laws and policies in accordance with the Charities Code.

39. Charities must abide by the provisions of the Charities Act 1994. For example, governing board members of a charity must ensure that accounting records that show and explain all the charity's transactions must be kept.[60] Such records must be preserved for at least five years after the end of the financial year in which the transaction was made.[61] Failure to do so can open the offender to an offence for which he/she can be punished with a fine, imprisonment or both.[62] The Commissioner of Charities can demand any person to furnish information or

56. Code of Governance for Registered Societies (June 2015), Art. 2.
57. Societies Act 1966, s. 10.
58. *Ibid.*, s. 12.
59. Code of Governance for Charities and Institutions of a Public Character (April 2017), Introduction.
60. Charities Act 1994, s. 11(1).
61. *Ibid.*, s. 11(3).
62. *Ibid.*, s. 16.

documentation relating to the charity; failure to do so can amount to an offence punishable by a fine, imprisonment or both.[63]

C. *Governing Instruments*

40. In order for an NSA to be registered as a charity it must have governing instruments. The governing instruments must set out the NSA's purposes, which must be exclusively charitable.[64] According to a guide published by the office of the Commissioner of Charities,[65] the basic requirements for the governing instruments include the following:

- the objects, which must be exclusively charitable for the public benefit, must be clearly and concisely stated;
- there should be at least three governing board members, who include Board Members, Management Committee Members and Directors;
- the duties, terms of office, appointment and removal procedures of the governing board members should be specified;
- there should be proper procedures in place to manage conflict of interest;
- the number of governing board members present to form a quorum for any meetings should be clearly stated;
- the circumstances under which the charity can be dissolved/wound up should be clearly stated.

41. Not all of the Constitutions for the various NSAs in Singapore are publicly available. A few examples of NSAs that have published their Constitutions online include the Football Association of Singapore (FAS),[66] the Singapore Table Tennis Association (STTA),[67] the Singapore Swimming Association,[68] the Singapore Sailing Federation,[69] the Singapore Shooting Association,[70] the Singapore Badminton Association,[71] the Singapore Golf Association,[72] the Singapore Ice Skating Association[73] and the Singapore Hockey Federation.[74]

---

63. *Ibid.*, s. 44.
64. Charities (Registration of Charities) Regulations, r. 3(1)(a).
65. Accessible at https://www.charities.gov.sg/Pages/Charities-and-IPCs/Register-as-a-Charity/Drafting-Your-GoverningInstrument.aspx (accessed 22 Nov. 2023).
66. Accessible at http://www.fas.org.sg/wp-content/uploads/2017/12/FAS-Constitution.pdf (accessed on 25 Feb. 2019).
67. Accessible at http://www.stta.org.sg/wp-content/uploads/2018/06/STTA-Constitution-Approved-14-Nov16_0.pdf (accessed on 25 Feb. 2019).
68. Accessible at http://www.swimming.org.sg/getattachment/SSA/ABOUT-US/Committee-Constitution/Constitution-Singapore-Swimming-Association-(as-of-21Aug2018).pdf.aspx (accessed on 25 Feb. 2019).
69. Accessible at https://sailing.org.sg/wp-content/uploads/2020/09/SSF-Constitution-min.pdf (accessed on 22 Nov. 2023).
70. Accessible at https://singaporeshooting.org/portal/about-us/ssa-constitution/ (accessed on 25 Feb. 2019).
71. Accessible at https://singaporebadminton.org.sg/sba-constitution/ (accessed on 22 Nov. 2023).
72. Accessible at https://www.sga.org.sg/about/constitution/ (accessed on 27 Feb. 2019).
73. Accessible at https://www.sisa.org.sg/assets/SISACon.pdf (accessed on 22 Nov. 2023).

42. The NSAs' governing instruments are not wholly identical. Provisions that are typically inserted include those relating to the NSA's objects, membership, membership fees, the end date for each financial year, the composition of the Management Committee (sometimes called the Executive Committee[75]), the duties and powers of the Management Committee, voting, election, general meetings, quorum and dissolution.

43. Provisions that may or may not be inserted into the NSAs' governing instruments include (but are not limited to) provisions relating to the NSA's colours, a policy regarding participation in overseas competitions, press releases and prohibition of betting or gambling.

D. Tax

44. Registered charities enjoy automatic income tax exemption under section 13(1)(zm) of the Income Tax Act 1947 and thus need not file income tax returns. However, they are required to register for goods and services tax if their annual taxable supplies exceed SGD 1 million even if they are engaged mostly in non-business activities. Taxable supplies include grants, donations and sponsorships where benefits are provided to the giver/donor in return for the sum of money or goods/services.

45. For societies where more than 50% of the gross revenue receipts on revenue accounts are from members, the society is not deemed to be carrying on a business. However, it will be liable to tax on income from other sources derived from dealings with non-members such as interest, rent and dividends. Where less than 50% of the gross revenue receipts on revenue accounts are from members, the society is deemed to be carrying on a business. It will be taxed on its operating surplus (total receipts of income less tax-deductible operating expenses), in addition to the income from other sources derived from dealings with non-members such as interest, rent and dividends.

E. Influence of SportSG

46. SportSG is the body that officially recognises organisations as NSAs. It also provides funding to a majority of NSAs.[76] As such, SportSG wields an enormous

74. Accessible at http://www.singaporehockey.org/wp-content/uploads/2017/08/SHF-Constitution-20141.pdf (accessed on 27 Feb. 2019).
75. For example, as named by the Singapore Swimming Association and the Singapore Sailing Federation.
76. Ms Grace Fu Hai Yien (8 May 2017), *Singapore Parliamentary Report vol. 94*, col. 29, available at https://sprs.parl.gov.sg/search/#/sprs3topic?reportid=written-answer-na-3531 (accessed 25 Feb. 2019).

amount of influence of sports in Singapore. Breach of the Charities Code or Societies Code may result in a reduction in priority status for funding, as well as a reduction in the amount of funding. If an NSA is found to be guilty of mismanagement or internal wrongdoing, it may even be stripped of its NSA status.

47. For example, in August 2002, the Singapore Sports Council (as SportSG was then named) (hereinafter 'SSC')suspended funding to the Singapore Tenpin Bowling Congress (hereinafter 'STBC'), due to ongoing investigations by the Commercial Affairs Department of the Singapore Police Force into the misappropriation of large sums from the STBC by its then-chief.[77] This was followed by the SSC forming a Bowling Review Committee in September 2002 to take over several key functions of the STBC for a reported period of four to twelve months. The committee was granted powers over fund management, team selection and major games preparation for bowlers in Singapore.[78]

48. In July 2004, the NSA for sepak takraw had its Merit status revoked by the SSC for failing to comply with the SSC's then-Code of Governance (now superseded by the Charities Code), which was an agreement between SSC and the NSAs to run their organisations professionally. The sepak takraw NSA was deemed to have run afoul of the provision that NSAs must have 'democratic and fair elections and appointments', by allowing voting rights to both appointed and outgoing members. A consequence of losing Merit status meant a decrease in funding, from a sum of up to SGD 2 million a year to a sum of up to only SGD 500,000 a year.[79] It was also reported that in April 2004, the NSAs for taekwondo and hockey had lost their Merit status because of poor performance.[80]

49. Later that same month, the sepak takraw NSA announced that it was ready to comply with the SSC's Code of Governance. No reason was given for its previous non-compliance. It also announced that after it regained its Merit status, it would apply for the maximum SGD 2 million grant, with the money intended to go towards improving the sports, and the national team and Under-eighteen team which had both won gold medals at recent regional competitions.[81]

50. In August 2013, the Singapore Bodybuilding Federation (hereinafter 'SBBF') became the first NSA to have its NSA status revoked by the SSC. This was

---

77. Tan, Nicholas (16 May 2016), *SportSG Happy to Help Floorball Put Its House in Order*, The Straits Times, https://www.straitstimes.com/sport/sportsg-happy-to-help-floorball-put-its-house-in-order (accessed 25 Jul. 2018).
78. Phang, Kelvin (12 Sep. 2002), *SSC Takes Charge of Bowling, Today*, http://eresources.nlb.gov.sg/newspapers/Digitised/Article/today20020912-1.2.54.7 (accessed 25 Jul. 2018).
79. Shing Huei, Peh (3 Jul. 2004), *SSC Axes Takraw from List of Merit Sports*, The Straits Times (accessible at National Library Board, Lee Kong Chian Reference Library, microfilm, reel number NL25630).
80. *Ibid.*
81. Lim, Marc (31 Jul. 2004), *Perses Ready to Comply*, The Straits Times (accessible at National Library Board, Lee Kong Chian Reference Library, microfilm, reel number NL25635).

the culmination of several events, including a 2012 revelation that the SBBF's President was an undischarged bankrupt and the August 2012 banning of seven SBBF members for doping offences.[82] SSC's Chief of Sports Development Group was quoted as saying, 'The leadership of SBBF has consistently shown its inability to lead the sport of bodybuilding – morally and operationally. The blatant doping violations and administrative incompetence has caused fragmentation within the bodybuilding fraternity. This decision is made to start to restore credibility and to rebuild the sport of bodybuilding.'[83]

F. Internal Discipline

51. Under the terms of the Societies Code, internal disputes are to be managed by the society.[84] Internal rules, regulations and codes of conduct of each NSA may provide for the liability of members, managers and officials if certain obligations or duties are not carried out, or if a person acts out of line. Disciplinary hearings may be held by internal tribunals and sanctions may be thereafter meted out against offenders.

52. For example, in December 2007, the FAS imposed a fine on a football player and banned him for twelve months for attacking another player on the pitch during a football final.[85] Other football brawls in 2010, 2016 and 2017 have seen players being banned and/or fined.[86] The FAS has also suspended teams from competitions after on-pitch brawls.[87]

53. In May 2010, a national badminton player was handed a three-month suspension without pay by the Singapore Badminton Association for displaying a poor attitude in training and tournaments and for failing to carry out instructions from her coach. In January 2011, she was again suspended for breaking curfew and

---

82. SportSG (7 Aug. 2012), *Two-Year Ban for Seven Bodybuilding Athletes Who Tested Positive for Prohibited Substances*, https://www.sportsingapore.gov.sg/newsroom/media-releases/2012/8/two-year-ban-for-seven-bodybuilding-athletes-who-tested-positive-for-prohibited-substances (accessed 24 Jul. 2018).
83. SportSG (16 Aug. 2013), *SBBF's NSA Status Revoked*, https://www.sportsingapore.gov.sg/newsroom/media-releases/2013/8/sbbf--nsa-status-revoked (accessed 24 Jul. 2018).
84. Code of Governance for Registered Societies (June 2015), Art. 4a.
85. Low, Lin Fhoong (18 Dec. 2007), *No Appeal, as Alam Shah Looks Overseas for Game Time*, Today, p. 1.
86. Lee, David (14 Nov. 2017), *Football: Police Investigating Sunday's Brawl Between Safsa and Yishun Sentek Mariners*, The Straits Times, https://www.straitstimes.com/sport/football/football-police-investigating-sundays-brawl-between-safsa-and-yishun-sentek-mariners (accessed 24 Jul. 2018); and Football Association of Singapore (31 Jan. 2018), *FAS Disciplinary Committee Reaches Verdict Case Involving Yishun Sentek Mariners FC and SAFSA*, http://www.fas.org.sg/announcement/fas-disciplinary-committee-reaches-verdict-case-involving-yishun-sentek-mariners-fc-and-safsa/ (accessed 24 Jul. 2018).
87. Football Association of Singapore, *NFL Team And Players Sanctioned For Misconduct And Bringing The Game Into Disrepute*, https://www.fas.org.sg/nfl-team-and-players-sanctioned-for-misconduct-and-bringing-the-game-into-disrepute/.

subsequently dropped from the national squad and barred from all training sessions. Matters came to a head in March 2011, when she was informed that her contract would not be renewed.[88]

54. In October 2016, a national table tennis player was sacked by the STTA for violating dormitory and house rules. He had falsified records of meal consumption in December 2015 and had allowed a woman to stay overnight at the STTA hostel on several occasions. The player had been given more than one verbal warning but had continued to flout the rules.[89]

55. In March 2017, a football player made comments on social media about a referee. The FAS Disciplinary Committee ordered him to provide a written apology to the referee and handed him a suspended fine.[90]

56. On 12 November 2017, a brawl erupted in the last ten minutes of a football match. At least eight players from the team Yishun Sentek Mariners, and another three players from the opposing team Singapore Armed Forces Sports Association, were involved. The FAS fined the Yishun club SGD 5,000. Its eight players were fined between SGD 300 and SGD 1,000 and given suspensions ranging between four and fifteen months. Of the three Singapore Armed Forces players, two were each given a four-month suspension and a fine of SGD 300, whereas the third received a stern warning.[91]

57. Officials may also be punished for infractions. For example, in February 2017, a fight broke out between a media officer from the FAS and a videographer. The FAS suspended the media officer from Singapore League games until the completion of the internal disciplinary committee investigation.[92]

58. On 15 January 2019, it was reported[93] that the FAS had terminated the employment of one of its employees over the violation of its financial governance

88. Wong, Jonathan (24 Mar. 2011), *Zhang 'Sacked' by SBA*, The Straits Times (accessible at National Library Board, Lee Kong Chian Reference Library, microfilm, reel number NL31298).
89. Wong, Jonathan (24 Oct. 2016), *Table Tennis: National Player Li Hu Sacked by STTA over Disciplinary Violation*, The Straits Times, https://www.straitstimes.com/sport/table-tennis-national-player-li-hu-sacked-by-stta-over-disciplinary-violation (accessed 24 Jul. 2018); and *Public Prosecutor v. Su Fengxian* [2018] SGDC 40 (Su had attempted to bribe a STTA official to induce him to be lenient to the player, who was her son).
90. Abdul Aziz, Sazali (17 Mar. 2017), *Suspended Fine for Madhu, Raihan Hearing Adjourned*, The New Paper, https://www.tnp.sg/sports/singapore-football/suspended-fine-madhu-raihan-hearing-adjourned (accessed 24 Jul. 2018).
91. Mohamed Shamir Mohamed Osman (9 Nov. 2018), *Court Fines Yishun Player $4,000 for Role in Brawl*, The Straits Times, https://www.straitstimes.com/sport/football/court-fines-yishun-player-4000-for-role-in-brawl (accessed 9 Nov. 2018).
92. Meng Meng, Wang (9 Mar. 2017), *Football: FAS Looking into Scuffle Between Media Officer and Videographer*, The Straits Times, https://www.straitstimes.com/sport/football/fas-looking-into-scuffle (accessed 25 Jul. 2018).
93. Mohamed Shamir Mohamed Osman (15 Jan. 2019), *Football: FAS Employee Sacked over Breach of Financial Protocols*, The Straits Times, https://www.straitstimes.com/sport/football/fas-employee-sacked-over-breach-of-financial-protocols (accessed 15 Jan. 2019).

protocols. The employee had admitted to a conflict of interest by getting the FAS to procure products and services from a vendor that was connected to the employee.

G. Recourse to the Courts

59. Where the NSA has rules and regulations that provide for internal dispute resolution, these internal processes must be exhausted before the matter is brought to the courts. Otherwise, the case may be struck out for abuse of process.

60. As sports disputes are often first dealt with under the internal processes of the respective NSA, there is a chance that inconsistencies and arbitrariness may arise. It is imperative that the internal disciplinary tribunal act in an impartial and reasonable manner. Otherwise, the decision may be challenged in Court.

61. An example of a sports tribunal breaching the rules of natural justice is the case of *Singapore Amateur Athletics Association v. Haron bin Mundir* [1993] 3 SLR(R) 407. The respondent was an athlete who was sent by his NSA (i.e., the appellant) for an overseas training trip. The respondent returned prematurely without the appellant's permission, and the appellant commenced disciplinary proceedings against him for misbehaviour. The respondent was suspended from competition for eighteen months. The respondent brought an action alleging that the appellant and its disciplinary subcommittee acted improperly and with malice in the disciplinary proceedings against him and that the proceedings had been conducted unfairly. The trial judge found in the respondent's favour, deciding that the appellant had acted in breach of the rules of natural justice in their conduct of the disciplinary proceedings and ordering that the decision for suspension be nullified. The appellant appealed to the Court of Appeal and lost. In dismissing the appeal, the Court of Appeal held that the preferred approach to the rules of natural justice was that of a duty to act fairly. The respondent was not adequately informed of the case he had to meet, nor was he truly given a reasonable opportunity to be heard, and thus, the respondent could not be said to have been afforded a fair hearing by the appellants' disciplinary subcommittee.

62. In *Ng Gino Ernest v. Triathlon Association of Singapore* [2007] SGHC 183, the applicant-athlete applied for leave for judicial review of a decision made by the respondent to nominate a fellow athlete for the national team of triathletes in the 2007 Southeast Asian Games. The applicant was not nominated and argued that he should have been nominated instead of his teammate. One of the grounds raised by the respondent for his application was that two members of the respondent's Appeals Committee were party to or were involved in the respondent's original decision to nominate the teammate. As such, these two members had judged their own decisions. The High Court of Singapore held that the applicant had sufficiently made out a case which required a response and granted leave to the applicant to bring a judicial review of the Appeals Committee's decision. Thereafter, parties resolved their differences through mediation,[94] and the appellant was nominated to represent Singapore at the said Games.

H. Arbitration

63. In January 2008, the SSC launched the Framework for Alternative Dispute Resolution for Sports (hereinafter 'ADR Sports') to resolve sports disputes. The aim of ADR Sports is to 'resolve problems faced by NSAs in areas such as athlete selections, discipline and contractual disputes'.[95] The intention is that resolution first be sought through the internal processes of the NSAs. Should this fail, the parties can refer the matter to ADR Sports for mediation and arbitration. It is compulsory for all NSAs to adopt ADR Sports.

64. Under the terms of the Memorandum of Understanding that was signed between the SSC, the Singapore International Arbitration Centre, the Singapore Mediation Centre and the Singapore Institute of Arbitrators, it was agreed that the latter three entities would provide arbitration and mediation services for sports-related cases, including (a) appointment of sports arbitrators and mediators; (b) institution of separate rules and/or standard operating procedures for the administration of sports-related cases, where applicable; and (c) designing and conducting training programmes to enhance awareness or knowledge on sports mediation/arbitration.[96]

65. However, in reality, ADR Sports has not been used often by parties who are unable to resolve disputes within their NSA. Judicial review continues to remain the primary means of challenging sanctions and non-selections.

94. Speech by Mr Teo Ser Luck, Parliamentary Secretary, Ministry of Community Development, Youth & Sports, at the launch of the Framework for Alternative Dispute Resolution for Sports (7 Jan. 2008), https://www.sportsingapore.gov.sg/newsroom/media-releases/2008/1/alternative-dispute-resolution-framework-for-sports-formed-to-resolve-disputes (accessed 24 Jul. 2018).

95. SportSG (7 Jan. 2008), *Alternative Dispute Resolution Framework for Sports Formed to Resolve Disputes*, https://www.sportsingapore.gov.sg/media-centre/media-release/alternative-dispute-resolution-framework-for-sports-formed-to-resolve/ (accessed 22 Nov. 2023).

96. Presentation slides on ADR Sports by Ho Mun Wai (7 Jan. 2008), https://www.sportsingapore.gov.sg/files/Media%20Centre/Media%20Release/2008/January/07/Annex20B2020Presentation20by20Mr20Ho20Mun20Wai20DPPM20SSCpptv2.pdf (accessed 22 Nov. 2023).

Chapter 2. Sports and Criminal Law

66. Behaviour on a sports ground may be regulated internally by the NSAs, but this does not mean that no criminal liability will fall on the parties involved. In the sports arena, several types of offences might arise. The most common type of offence is that involving the causing of hurt to another person. Other offences that have been prosecuted include match-fixing, the misappropriation of a sports entity's funds and sexual abuse by coaches or instructors of their athletes.

§1. Reporting Obligations

67. Generally, there is no obligation to report a crime unless the crime is one of those listed in section 424 of the Criminal Procedure Code 2010 (hereinafter 'CPC'). The provisions specified in section 424 relate to offences against the State, offences relating to the armed forces, offences relating to unlawful assembly, offences relating to coin and Government stamps, offences affecting the human body (including murder, rape, causing miscarriage, causing bodily hurt, wrongful confinement, assault, kidnapping, sexual assault and commercial sex with minors), offences relating to public servants, extortion, robbery, mischief, trespass, forgery of currency notes or bank notes and criminal intimidation.

68. No punishment is prescribed for a breach of section 424 of the CPC. There is also no reported case in Singapore regarding the consequences of breaching section 424.

69. Section 45 of the Corruption, Drug Trafficking and Other Serious Crimes (Confiscation of Benefits) Act 1992 (hereinafter 'CDSA') imputes an obligation on a person to lodge a Suspicious Transaction Report (hereinafter 'STR') if he knows or has reasonable grounds to suspect that any property represents the proceeds of, was used in connection with, or is intended to be used in connection with, an act that may constitute drug dealing or criminal conduct, and the person's knowledge or suspicion is based on information that came to his attention in the course of his business or employment. This obligation may arise in situations where monies have been misappropriated from a sports body, or in situations where drugs are passed to athletes for consumption.

70. Section 45(3) of the CDSA makes it clear that failure to file an STR when the obligation arises exposes the person who fails to file the STR to criminal liability. If found guilty, the person may be liable to a fine of up to SGD 250,000 or to imprisonment for a term not exceeding three years or both.

71. If an STR is filed, care ought to be taken not to infringe the 'tipping-off' provision under section 57 of the CDSA (e.g., by informing the subject of the STR that an STR has been filed). Under section 57(1), where a person knows or has reasonable grounds to suspect that an officer from the STR Office is acting or proposing to act in connection with an investigation, that person must not disclose to any other person information or any other matter which is likely to prejudice the investigation. Furthermore, under section 57(2), where a person knows or has reasonable grounds to suspect that a disclosure has been made to the STR Office, that person must not disclose to any other person information or any other matter which is likely to prejudice any investigation which might be conducted following the disclosure. Infringement of each provision amounts to a criminal offence, punishable upon conviction with a fine of up to SGD 250,000, or imprisonment for a term not exceeding three years, or both.

§2. Procedure for Investigations and Prosecution

72. Once a First Information Report is filed (e.g., by a concerned member of the public or by a victim), the police are obliged to commence and carry out investigations.[97] The police have powers to require production of any document or any other thing,[98] to require the attendance of a witness who appears to be acquainted with any of the facts and circumstances of the case[99] and to interview the witness and record a statement.[100] This statement is colloquially known as a 'section 22 statement', an 'investigation statement' or a 'long statement'. The police will not give the witness a copy of such statement.

73. Upon the conclusion of investigations, the investigation papers are handed over to the Attorney-General's Chambers for review. The Attorney-General is the Public Prosecutor, and he or any Deputy Public Prosecutor has the control and direction of all criminal prosecutions and proceedings in Singapore.[101] Discretion as to whether to charge any person, and the type and number of charges involved, lies solely in the hands of the Attorney-General's Chambers, although recommendations by the investigation officer can be taken into account.

74. In the event that a person is charged, the charge(s) will be read out to the person by a police officer. The accused person will be invited to provide a written cautioned statement in respect of each charge levied against him.[102] The accused person can either respond in writing to the charge or refuse to respond. Any such refusal will be noted in writing in the cautioned statement papers. A copy of the cautioned statement will be given to the accused person. The accused person will then be given a date and time on which to attend court. At court, the accused person can indicate his intention as to how he wishes to proceed with his case.

75. If the accused person claims trial, and if he is charged for an offence that falls within the ambit of the statutes listed in the Second Schedule of the CPC, then

97. CPC, ss 16 and 17.
98. *Ibid.*, s. 20.
99. *Ibid.*, s. 21.
100. *Ibid.*, s. 22.
101. *Ibid.*, s. 11.
102. *Ibid.*, s. 23.

the Prosecution is obliged to furnish him with a copy of his section 22 statement during the pretrial disclosure procedure (known as the 'Criminal Case Disclosure Procedure').[103] In all other situations, there is no statutory obligation on the Prosecution to furnish a copy of the section 22 statement to the accused person.

76. In the decision of *Muhammad bin Kadar and another v. Public Prosecutor* [2011] 3 SLR 1205 (hereinafter '*Kadar*'), the Singapore Court of Appeal held that the Prosecution is required to disclose to the Defence material which takes the form of: (a) any unused material that is likely to be admissible and might reasonably be regarded as credible and relevant to the guilt or innocence of the accused person; and (b) any unused material that is likely to be inadmissible but would provide a real (not fanciful) chance of pursuing a line of inquiry that leads to material that is likely to be admissible and that might reasonably be regarded as credible and relevant to the guilt or innocence of the accused person (at [113]). Such disclosure obligations do not cover materials that are neutral or adverse to the accused person.

77. In *Xu Yuanchen v. Public Prosecutor and another matter* [2021] SGHC 64, the accused persons filed interlocutory applications seeking the disclosure of their section 22 statements pursuant to the Prosecution's common law disclosure obligations as set out in *Kadar*. The applications were dismissed during trial. The accused persons then filed criminal motions seeking production of the statements. The Singapore High Court dismissed the applications, noting that they were barred for being procedurally defective owing to the fact that they were effectively appeals against interlocutory rulings. Nevertheless, the Court went on to consider the substantive issue. It held that the *Kadar* disclosure obligations had not been triggered since there was no indication that the section 22 statements would assist the Defence or weaken the Prosecution's case.[104] There was no material before the Court to cast doubt on the Prosecution's assessment that the material in question did not come within the ambit of its *Kadar* disclosure obligations. Furthermore, given that the accused persons had brought their applications when the Prosecution had not yet closed its case at trial, the accused persons could not point to any particular injustice that had been or would be occasioned by the denial of their section 22 statements at that stage.[105] In a final coda, the Court observed that an accused person's own statements, being a form of evidence that emanates entirely from the accused person, may not properly fall within the universe of unused evidentiary material that the *Kadar* disclosure obligations are intended to address.[106] Nevertheless, the Court left this point for consideration should the question come before the Singapore Court of Appeal in the future.[107]

103. *Ibid.*, s. 159.
104. *Xu Yuanchen v. Public Prosecutor and another matter* [2021] SGHC 64, at para. 35.
105. *Ibid.*, at para. 37.
106. *Ibid.*, at para. 43.
107. *Ibid.*, at para. 44.

§3. Offences Involving Violence

78. Offences that involve violent acts can range in terms of the amount of harm caused to the victim. The acts may occur during a match or competition, or may occur outside the sport grounds but arise from a dispute that took place during a sports event. Such offences generally fall under the Penal Code 1871 (hereinafter 'Penal Code'). Applicable provisions include:

- Section 143: unlawful assembly.
- Section 147: rioting.
- Section 148: rioting armed with deadly weapon.
- Section 302: murder.
- Section 304: culpable homicide not amounting to murder.
- Section 304A: causing death by rash or negligent act.
- Section 323: voluntarily causing hurt.
- Section 324: voluntarily causing hurt by dangerous weapon or means.
- Section 325: voluntarily causing grievous hurt.
- Section 326: voluntarily causing grievous hurt by dangerous weapon or means.
- Section 352: using criminal force otherwise than on grave and sudden provocation.

79. An example of on-pitch violence between players is found in *Public Prosecutor v. Newley William Michael Irvin* [2002] SGDC 159. The offender and the victim were on opposing teams playing football. In the course of the match, the victim was tackled by the offender's teammate. The offender's teammate was sent off by the referee. The victim was restrained by his own teammates to prevent him from retaliating. At that juncture, the offender headbutted the victim on the nose, causing bleeding and a nasal fracture. The offender was charged under section 323 of the Penal Code and penalised with a one-month imprisonment term. The offender filed an appeal against his sentence but eventually allowed his appeal to lapse.[108]

80. Public Prosecutor v. Gan Boon Kheng [2016] SGDC 162 presents another example. The offender and the victim were playing on opposite sides during a basketball game when a dispute over a foul arose between their respective teammates. A disagreement then ensued between the offender and the victim, resulting in the offender punching the victim. The victim suffered nasal fractures. The offender was charged under section 323 of the Penal Code. He was sentenced to a fourteen-day short detention order and further ordered to perform 110 hours of community service within one year.

81. On 12 November 2017, an on-pitch melee ensued between players of two football teams. One of the players was charged under section 323 of the Penal Code

108. The lapse of the appeal was noted by the judge in *Quek Kheok Seng v. Public Prosecutor* [2003] SGDC 198, at para. 28.

for delivering a flying kick to another player's upper torso. He pleaded guilty and was sentenced to a fine of SGD 4,000.[109]

82. Violence may also take place between a player and a referee. In *Public Prosecutor v. Muhammad Maziz Bin Abdul Rahman,*[110] the victim was a referee in a football match where the offender was a player. The victim gave the offender two yellow cards and a red card. Infuriated, the offender rushed towards the victim and stepped on the victim's foot with his football boot. The offender also lunged his boot into the victim's thigh and punched the victim on his eye and nose. The offender was convicted and sentenced to ten months' imprisonment, with a compensation order for SGD 2,000 to be paid to the victim.[111] In terms of internal discipline, the offender was given a five-year ban by the FAS.[112]

83. On-field rage may on occasion flare up into violence off-field. In *Public Prosecutor v. Indra bin Mohamed Sharum* [2005] SGDC 7, a dispute occurred on a football pitch between two players. Later that same day, the players had a confrontation at a bus interchange, during which the victim was present. The victim was a friend of one of the two players. The next day, the other player rounded up friends, including the offender. They armed themselves with weapons and then attacked the victim. The victim was knifed during the attack by the offender, who was charged under section 148 of the Penal Code. The court took into account that the victim suffered serious injuries and that the attack had been brazen and blatant, taking place at 12 noon at a crowded coffee shop. The offender was convicted and sentenced to an imprisonment term of three years, with six strokes of the cane.

84. In rare situations, unhappiness between players during a game may culminate in a fatality. In *Mohamed Salleh v. Public Prosecutor* [1968-1970] SLR(R) 330, the offender and the deceased were playing football when the deceased called the offender a bastard. After the game, the offender brooded over what the deceased had said. He subsequently located a knife and plunged it into the deceased four times. The offender was charged and convicted of murder. The mandatory sentence of capital punishment was subsequently carried out.

85. Similarly, in *Mohamad Yassin bin Jappar v. Public Prosecutor* [1994] 3 SLR(R) 17, the offender and the deceased had a disagreement over a game of table tennis. After the game, the offender stabbed the deceased. He claimed that he had only intended to hurt, not kill, the deceased because the deceased had embarrassed him in front of others. Nevertheless, the trial judge found that the offender had

---

109. Mohamed Shamir Mohamed Osman (9 Nov. 2018), *Court fines Yishun player $4,000 for role in brawl*, The Straits Times, https://www.straitstimes.com/sport/football/court-fines-yishun-player-4000-for-role-in-brawl (accessed 9 Nov. 2018).

110. District Arrest Case 902960 of 2015 (unreported).

111. The facts are available at para. 26 of *Public Prosecutor v. Mohamed Razalli Bin Husin* [2017] SGDC 117.

112. *See* the FAS *List of Suspended Players/Officials for 2017(Carried over to 2018)*, http://www.fas.org.sg/wp-content/uploads/2018/07/FAS-Midnight-Football-Challenge-2017-Suspensions-for-2018.pdf.

intended to inflict the injury that had led to the deceased's death, i.e., a neck wound. The offender was thus convicted of murder.

86. Sports participants are not the only ones who may be caught up in violence. On 4 August 2022, the FAS Disciplinary Committee found a head coach and an assistant coach guilty of charges for violent conduct, following a head-butting incident on the field.[113] Both men were fined and given a three-match suspension.[114] Their respective teams were also fined for not controlling their officials in an orderly manner during a match.

87. Additionally, unruly spectators may resort to violence and find themselves before the courts. For example, during the Tiger Cup semi-finals between Singapore and Myanmar held at Singapore's National Stadium in January 2005, several on-pitch incidents saw the number of Myanmar team players reduced to eight. The Singapore team eventually won four-two. After the match, spectators from the rival nations fought outside the stadium. Those involved were arrested, charged and convicted under the Penal Code.

88. Even third-party bystanders may become embroiled in violence. In *Public Prosecutor v. Tan Chee Siang Keith*,[115] the victim, aged 9, was playing football with a friend. The victim kicked the ball, and it accidentally struck the offender's daughter, who was passing by on her skate scooter. She fell off her skate scooter and started crying. To teach the victim a lesson, the offender made the victim stand 1 metre from a wall, facing the wall. The offender then kicked the football against the victim's legs four times. On one occasion, the football missed the victim's legs, rebounded off the wall, and hit the victim in the face, causing a nosebleed. The offender was fined and ordered to pay compensation to the victim.

§4. Sexual Offences

89. Sexual offences in the sports industry are unfortunately not uncommon. Recent notable cases include the 2017/18 conviction of former USA Gymnastics national team doctor Larry Nassar, who was accused of sexually assaulting more

113. Football Association of Singapore (4 Aug. 2022), *Disciplinary Committee Hearing on Case Involving Lion City Sailors FC and Tampines Rovers FC*, https://www.fas.org.sg/disciplinary-committee-hearing-on-case-involving-lion-city-sailors-fc-and-tampines-rovers-fc/ (accessed 29 Nov. 2023).
114. Football Association of Singapore (10 Aug. 2022), *FAS Disciplinary Committee Reaches Verdict on Case Involving Lion City Sailors FC and Tampines Rovers FC*, https://www.fas.org.sg/fas-disciplinary-committee-reaches-verdict-on-case-involving-lion-city-sailors-fc-and-tampines-rovers-fc/ (accessed 29 Nov. 2023).
115. Magistrates Case Number 909324 of 2016 (reported by Chong, Elena (6 Dec. 2016), *Stockbroker Fined $2,000 for Kicking Football Against Boy's Legs 3 Times*, The Straits Times, https://www.straitstimes.com/singapore/courts-crime/stockbroker-fined-2k-for-kicking-football-against-boys-legs-three-times (accessed 15 Jan. 2019)).

than 250 young girls, including several famous Olympic gymnasts. In 2012, Pennsylvania State University assistant coach Jerry Sandusky was found guilty of several charges of sexual abuse of young boys. In the United Kingdom, investigations into non-recent sexual abuse of young players at football clubs have been ongoing since November 2016.

90. Singapore has also seen its share of cases involving sexual abuse of athletes by coaches. If no police report is filed, the case may be handled internally. For example, in July 2022, it was reported that a coach at a private football academy was fired after sending a lewd photograph to two teenage players under his charge. It was also reported that no report to the police or Safe Sport Commission had been lodged;[116] the academy is not a member of the Safe Sport programme, and the coach involved was not registered with the NROC.[117]

91. If the cases proceed to court, charges are typically brought under one or more of the following provisions of the Penal Code:

- Section 354: use of criminal force with intent to outrage modesty.
- Section 375: rape.
- Section 376: sexual assault by penetration.
- Section 376A: sexual penetration of minor under 16.

92. Other statutory provisions under which criminal proceedings for sexual abuse may be brought include the following:

- Section 506 of the Penal Code: criminal intimidation (e.g., by threatening to post online or circulate sexually explicit photographs or videos of the victim).
- Section 7 of the Children and Young Persons Act 1993 (hereinafter 'CYPAct'): sexual exploitation of child or young person. A child is defined in section 2 of the CYPAct as a person who is below the age of 14. A young person is defined in the same section as a person who is at or above the age of 14 and below the age of 16.
- Section 140(1)(i) of the Women's Charter 1961: carnal connection with a girl below the age of 16.

93. Lee Kwang Peng v. Public Prosecutor [1997] 2 SLR(R) 569 involved an offender who claimed trial to nine charges under section 354 of the Penal Code. The offender was a taekwondo instructor. He faced allegations from three of his male teenage students, for fondling their genitals on separate occasions when he was

116. Sazali Abdul Aziz (31 Jul. 2022), *Coach at Private Football Academy in S'pore Sacked after Sending Lewd Photo to Female Teen Players*, The Straits Times, https://www.straitstimes.com/sport/football/football-coach-sacked-after-sending-lewd-photo-to-female-teen-players (accessed 23 Nov. 2023).
117. Sazali Abdul Aziz (10 Aug. 2022), *Football: Safe Sport Commission in Contact with Academy over Ex-Coach's Misconduct*, The Straits Times, https://www.straitstimes.com/sport/football/football-safe-sport-commission-in-contact-with-academy-over-ex-coachs-misconduct (accessed 23 Nov. 2023).

alone with them, sometimes on the pretext of checking for training injuries and sometimes without reasonable excuse. He was convicted at first instance and sentenced to four months' imprisonment per charge, with three sentences to run consecutively and the remainder to run concurrently, making it a total of twelve months' imprisonment. His appeal against conviction and sentence was dismissed by the appellate court. Instead, the appellate court allowed the Prosecution's cross-appeal on sentence, in view of the victims' ages, and the fact that the offender had abused the trust reposed in him by the victims and their parents. His sentence was increased to nine months' imprisonment, with two sentences to run consecutively and the remainder to run concurrently, thus making it a total of eighteen months' imprisonment.

94. In *Public Prosecutor v. Low Chuan Wee Anthony* [2011] SGHC 258, the offender was the female victim's martial arts instructor. The victim was aged about 13 at the material time. They entered into a consensual relationship and referred to each other as *lao gong* (Mandarin for 'husband') and *lao po* (Mandarin for 'wife') in their communications with each other. The offender also introduced the victim as his *lao po* to his friends. The relationship was eventually discovered by the victim's school, which then informed the victim's mother. The victim subsequently lodged a police report. The offender claimed trial to seven charges under section 376 of the Penal Code and section 7 of the CYPAct. He was convicted. In considering sentencing factors, the court noted that the victim was a willing party to events. However, she had been under the influence of a much older man who was in a position of trust and who had exploited the victim's interest in him. As such, he was sentenced to a global imprisonment term of eleven years, with twelve strokes of the cane.

95. In January 2016, a badminton coach who groomed his male student aged 14 and pressured him to engage in sexual activities was sentenced to five years' imprisonment.[118] In May 2017, a swimming coach was convicted under section 7 of the CYPAct for committing an obscene act with a boy aged 12 in a toilet cubicle at a swimming complex. He was sentenced to ten months' imprisonment.[119]

96. *Public Prosecutor v. Toh Leng Poh* [2018] SGDC 173 featured an offender who claimed trial to two charges under section 376A of the Penal Code. The offender was the male victim's basketball coach. The charges related to his fellating the victim and sodomising the victim, without the victim's consent. The victim filed a police report as he was concerned that he could have contracted a sexually transmitted disease. After convicting the offender, the court went on to consider the following aggravating sentencing factors that: (a) the offender had abused his position as the victim's coach and breached the victim's trust, (b) there was psychological

118. Chong, Elena (13 Jan. 2016), *Badminton coach sentenced to five years in jail for grooming boy for sex*, The Straits Times, https://www.straitstimes.com/singapore/courts-crime/badminton-coach-sentenced-to-five-years-in-jail-for-grooming-boy-for-sex (accessed 27 Jul. 2018).

119. Koh, Valerie (5 May 2017), *Swim Coach, 69, Gets Jail for Sexually Exploiting Boy*, Today, https://www.todayonline.com/singapore/swim-coach-69-gets-jail-sexually-exploiting-boy (accessed 27 Jul. 2018).

harm and physical pain caused to the victim and (c) there was a significant degree of exploitation as the offender had committed different types of penetrative acts against the victim. The offender was sentenced to a global sentence of ten years' imprisonment. As he was aged above 50, no sentence of caning was imposed.

97. In terms of egregiousness, *Public Prosecutor v. Yue Roger Jr* [2018] SGHC 125 falls on the higher end of the spectrum. The female victim was aged between 13 and 14 at the material time. The offender was the victim's rope-skipping coach, and they were in a romantic relationship at the material time. The offender was charged with forty-eight counts, of which seven were proceeded with at trial. These seven charges comprised offences under sections 375 and 376A of the Penal Code. One of the offences involved sexual penetration by a vibrator, and another involved sexual penetration by a skipping rope handle. The offender was convicted. In determining his sentence, the Singapore High Court noted that (a) the offender had abused his position as the victim's coach, (b) there was premeditation as the offender had taken steps to sexually groom the victim, (c) the sexual abuse took place over multiple occasions over an extended period of time and (d) the offender's failure to use condoms exposed the victim to the risk of pregnancy and sexually transmitted diseases. The offender was sentenced to a global sentence of twenty-five years' imprisonment. As he was aged above 50, no sentence of caning was imposed.

98. Cases involving pleas of guilt are not necessarily treated with a high level of leniency in terms of sentencing, as compared to cases when the offender claims trial. For example, in *Public Prosecutor v. Tan Meng Soon Bernard* [2018] SGHC 134, the offender was a football coach. He sexually abused five of his footballer players, who were all aged 12 or below. The offender pleaded guilty to five charges under section 375 of the Penal Code. He further consented to twenty other charges, which included seventeen charges under section 376 and section 376A of the Penal Code, being taken into consideration for sentencing purposes. The court took note of aggravating factors such as (a) the young age of the victims, (b) the abuse of trust placed in the offender by the victims and their parents and (c) the level of premeditation. The offender was sentenced to a global sentence of twenty-six years' imprisonment, with twenty-four strokes of the cane.

99. In May 2021, a sports coach was sentenced to a custodial term of thirty-one years and twenty-four strokes of the cane, for the rape of two minors aged 13 and 14.[120] He had become acquainted with one victim when he was engaged by a school to conduct activities for pupils and got her to rope her friend into his web. Both victims were tricked into participating in threesomes with him and engaging in various sexual acts.

---

120. Lum, Selina (25 May 2021), *Coach Who Duped 2 Underaged Girls into Having Sex with Him Gets 31 Years' Jail, Caning for Rape*, The Straits Times, https://www.straitstimes.com/singapore/courts-crime/coach-who-duped-2-underaged-girls-into-having-sex-with-him-gets-31-years-jail (accessed 27 May 2021).

100. In December 2022, a swimming coach with a paedophilic disorder who had sexually abused a student for four years pleaded guilty to five charges, including one count of sexual assault by penetration, three counts of aggravated outrage of modesty and one count of possession of obscene films. Another fifteen charges were taken into consideration for sentencing purposes. He was sentenced to eighteen years and eleven months' imprisonment, and twenty-one strokes of the cane.[121]

101. In order to prevent sexual abuse of athletes, sports bodies in Singapore have adopted various measures.[122] For example, a standard operating procedure at the NSA Singapore Gymnastics is that its coaches cannot be in the gymnasium on a one-on-one basis with athletes. At a particular swimming club, at least one coordinator must be present at each of the club's training sessions. For the STTA, managers and staff must be notified if individual training sessions are conducted. SingaporeSailing mandates that debriefs be held in groups and in a suitable location.

102. Coaches who wish to register under SportSG's NROC scheme must complete the Values and Principles in Sports course, which includes in its teachings the right of youths to play sports free of abuse.[123] All NROC-registered coaches are reminded in the Coach's Code of Ethics to avoid sexual intimacy with athletes and that physical contact with athletes should take place only when absolutely necessary and during appropriate situations.[124] Breach of the Coach's Code of Ethics may result in the NROC suspending the coach and the relevant NSA instituting disciplinary proceedings against the coach. However, registration in the NROC is not compulsory for coaches in Singapore, and thus not all coaches are bound by the Coach's Code of Ethics.

103. On 2 April 2018, SportSG, SNOC and fifty-seven NSAs issued a joint statement, pledging commitment against sexual harassment and inappropriate behaviour of any form in the sports fraternity.[125] The statement noted, 'Some preliminary actions to prevent harassment and protect the people are through education, information sharing, establishing best practices, and providing support to NSAs, including but not limited to, creating and distributing tool kits designed to empower them to take prompt and effective actions.'

---

121. Lum, Selina (2 Dec. 2022), *Swimming Coach Who Sexually Abused Student Gets Nearly 19 Years' Jail, Caning*, The Straits Times, https://www.straitstimes.com/singapore/courts-crime/swim-coach-who-sexually-abused-student-gets-nearly-19-years-jail-caning (accessed 22 Nov. 2023).
122. Chia, Nicole (3 Dec. 2017), *Sexual Abuse in Sports: How Sports Bodies Here Protect Their Athletes*, The Straits Times, https://www.straitstimes.com/sport/sexual-abuse-in-sports-how-sports-bodies-here-protect-their-athletes (accessed 27 Jul. 2018).
123. Ong, Justin (6 Jan. 2017), *Safeguards Against Child Sex Abuse in Sport Can Be Strengthened: Officials*, Channel NewsAsia, https://web.archive.org/web/20190901000000*/https://www.channelnewsasia.com/news/singapore/safeguards-against-child-sex-abuse-in-sport-can-be-strengthened--7533006 (accessed 27 Jul. 2018).
124. Coach's Code of Ethics, Art. 5.2.6.
125. SportSG (2 Apr. 2018), *Sport Bodies Say No to Sexual Misconduct in Singapore*, https://www.sportsingapore.gov.sg/newsroom/media-releases/2018/4/sport-bodies-say-no-to-sexual-misconduct-in-singapore (accessed 27 Jul. 2018).

104. Between 6 and 7 April 2018, representatives from SportSG attended the inaugural Safe Sport International Conference held in Madrid. The Conference addressed research evidence, policy responses, preventive strategies and the growing demand for safe sports practice to secure sports as a place of safety for all athletes.[126]

105. Subsequently, in May 2018, SportSG hosted the first Safe Sport Forum in Singapore, which was attended by representatives from NSAs, the SNOC, the Singapore Police Force, the Ministry of Education and the Ministry of Social and Family Development. The purpose of the Forum was to look into preventative measures to safeguard sports participants from sexual misconduct. During the Forum, SportSG committed to lead the prevention strategy and education effort by establishing a Safe Sport Commission and a reporting process by 2019. The NSAs also pledged to have a sport safe policy and a safeguarding officer by 2019, in order to provide a safe and trusted environment for staff, associates, athletes, coaches and officials in accordance with existing laws and codes of conduct.[127]

106. On 8 March 2021, the Minister for Culture, Community and Youth announced that a Safe Sport Programme would be established through the Safe Sport Commission:[128]

– First, to prevent inappropriate behaviour, a Unified Code will be developed to provide the sporting community with a shared reference point against inappropriate behaviour. The Unified Code will define the types of inappropriate behaviour, such as sexual misconduct and psychological and physical misconduct. The definitions are based on the principles set out in the IOC's Consensus Statement on Non-Accidental Violence in Sport. To contextualise these definitions to Singapore's culture and laws, the Unified Code will until September 2021 undergo a three-phased consultation with stakeholders in the community and experts in safeguarding.[129] Those being consulted include (to name a few) the Ministry of Social and Family Development, the Singapore Police Force, the Ministry of Education, the Association of Women for Action and Research, the SNOC, the Singapore National Paralympic Council, athletes, coaches, and sport administrators.[130]

---

126. Safe Sport International, *Eliminating Violence in Sport and Creating Safety for Athletes*, https://web.archive.org/web/20190418125124/http://www.safesportinternational.com/1st-international-conference-for-safe-sport/ (accessed 27 Jul. 2018).
127. SportSG (24 May 2018), *Singapore Hosts First Safe Sport Forum*, https://www.sportsingapore.gov.sg/newsroom/media-releases/2018/5/singapore-hosts-first-safe-sport-forum (accessed 27 Jul. 2018).
128. Mr Edwin Tong Chun Fai (8 Mar. 2021), *Singapore Parliamentary Report vol. 95*, sitting no. 27, https://sprs.parl.gov.sg/search/#/sprs3topic?reportid=budget-1638 (accessed 3 May 2021).
129. SportSG, *A Quick Guide to Safe Sport Unified Code*, https://www.sportsingapore.gov.sg/-/media/SSC/Corporate/Files/Athletes-and-Coaches/Safe-Sport/Quick-Guide-Safe-Sport-Unified-Code.pdf?la=en&hash=F60998B2E2855DE26D98319F080F88400DF613ED (accessed 3 May 2021).
130. SportSG, *Safe Sport Programme*, https://www.sportsingapore.gov.sg/athletes-coaches/safe-sport/safe-sport-programme (accessed 3 May 2021).

- Second, to address incidents, a confidential third-party reporting channel and enhanced case management will offer affected individuals access to reporting channels and support.
- Third, to assure participants, the Safe Sport Commission will introduce an accreditation framework. The criteria will be based on the adoption of the Unified Code, implementation of relevant policies and training of persons involved. Sports organisations that meet the criteria will be accredited through a Safe Sport Mark. This will help sports participants to easily identify sporting organisations that are committed to practising Safe Sport.

§5. Corruption

107. Corruption offences can take many forms, and involve athletes, family members of athletes, officials and referees. Despite a high Transparency International Rating of 85 of 100, and being ranked joint-third of 180 countries in the 2020 index,[131] Singapore has been associated with the fixing of football matches for several years. The authorities have sought to polish up Singapore's image by clamping down hard on match-fixers in recent years.

108. The primary source of Singapore's anti-corruption legislation is the Prevention of Corruption Act 1960 (hereinafter 'PCA'), which applies to both private and public sector corruption offences.

109. The key provisions of the PCA are sections 5 and 6, which make it an offence for a person (including an agent) to (a) corruptly solicit, receive, agree to receive, give, promise or offer gratification, (b) whether for his own benefit or for the benefit of another person, (c) as an inducement or reward for doing or forbearing to do anything in respect of any matter or transaction, actual or proposed.

110. As defined in section 2 of the PCA, 'gratification' can take various forms, including but not limited to: money; any gift, loan, fee, reward, commission, valuable security, property or interest in movable or immovable property, employment, contract, service, favour, advantage; and any offer, undertaking or promise of any of the aforementioned.

111. There is no exhaustive definition of a 'corrupt' transaction. To determine if a particular transaction is corrupt, the circumstances surrounding the provision of the benefit have to be examined. The courts will generally consider several factors, including:

- purpose behind the provision of the gratification;
- proximity of time between the act of the receiver and the giving of gratification;

131. Rating by Transparency International in its Corruption Perceptions Index 2020. This Index ranks countries and territories by their perceived levels of public sector corruption according to experts and business people and is not an index for private sector corruption.

- any furtiveness or surreptitious element in the transactions;
- nature and frequency of the gratification;
- quantum of gratification;
- relationship between the parties;
- whether there was any prior communication/solicitation before payment of gratification; and
- whether the recipient has in fact shown or has the power to show favour to the giver.

112. In assessing whether an offence of corruption has been committed under section 5 or 6 of the PCA, there must have been giving, promising or offering, or soliciting, accepting or agreeing to receive a gratification in the belief that it is meant as a quid pro quo for conferring a dishonest gain or advantage. There must be a corrupt element in the transaction according to the ordinary and objective standard, followed by the offender's guilty knowledge that what he was doing was, by that standard, corrupt. The standard of proof to sustain a conviction in a criminal case is that of beyond a reasonable doubt.

113. Section 8 of the PCA gives rise to a presumption of corruption; i.e., the Prosecution is presumed to have passed the test of corruption if the Prosecution can prove that gratification was paid or received by a public officer or a Government official (being a person in the employment of the Singapore Government or any department thereof or of a public body), by or from a person who at the time of the payment, gift or receipt had or sought to have dealings with the Singapore Government or that department of the Government or that public body.

114. In turn, a 'public body' is defined in section 2 of the PCA as any corporation, board, council, commissioners or other body which has the power to act under and for the purposes of any written law relating to public health or to undertakings or public utility or otherwise to administer money levied or raised by rates or charges in pursuance of any written law.

115. There is no statutory defence set out in the PCA to an allegation of corruption. In order to defeat a charge of corruption, one must show that (a) there was no gratification given, requested, offered or accepted; or (b) there was no corrupt element in the transaction according to the ordinary and objective standard; or (c) one did not have the requisite guilty knowledge that what he was doing was, by that standard, corrupt.

116. A person (which includes both individuals and corporate entities) found guilty of an offence under section 5 or section 6 of the PCA shall be liable to conviction to a fine not exceeding SGD 100,000, or to imprisonment for a term not exceeding five years, or to both. Should the offender be a corporate entity, only fines may be levied as punishment.

117. Pursuant to section 13 of the PCA, an offender who receives gratification may also be required to pay penalties equivalent to the amount of gratification received, in addition to the punishment imposed. The objective of section 13 is to disgorge from the offender his ill-gotten gains from the corrupt transactions.

118. Section 37 of the PCA expressly stipulates that its provisions extend to all offences committed outside Singapore if committed by citizens of Singapore. Where an offence under the PCA is committed by a citizen of Singapore in any place outside Singapore, he may be dealt with in respect of that offence as if it had been committed within Singapore. Section 37 is capable of capturing all corrupt acts by Singapore citizens outside Singapore, irrespective of whether or not such corrupt acts have consequences within the borders of Singapore.

119. A report alleging corruption by an individual and/or corporation may be filed with Singapore's Corrupt Practices Investigation Bureau (hereinafter 'CPIB'), which is the investigative authority for corruption cases. The CPIB has the same investigative powers as the police. In addition, under section 27 of the PCA, a person who is interviewed by the CPIB must give any information that is in his power to give; there is no right against self-incrimination.

I. Match-Fixing

120. In *Kannan s/o Kunjiraman and Another v. Public Prosecutor* [1995] 3 SLR(R) 294 (hereinafter '*PP v. Kannan*'), two offenders were charged under section 5 of the PCA. They were, respectively, a committee member and the President of a football club. Both conspired with a bookmaker to offer SGD 80,000 to the goalkeeper of Singapore's national football team to let in goals during a match. The President was to be the go-between to liaise with the goalkeeper but did not do so. As it turned out, the goalkeeper let goals in during the match. Thinking that the offenders had carried out their end of the deal, the bookkeeper gave the SGD 80,000 to the offenders. He also gave SGD 5,000 to the committee members as a reward. The President kept the SGD 80,000 for himself. The committee member was sentenced to eighteen months' imprisonment and ordered to pay a penalty of SGD 5,000. The President was sentenced to thirty months' imprisonment and ordered to pay a penalty of SGD 80,000. Both offenders filed appeals against their convictions and sentences, but their appeals were dismissed. Both offenders were also given a lifetime ban from the sport by the FAS.[132] Pursuant to the committee member's appeal, the ban against him was lifted in March 2022.[133]

121. The bookkeeper in *PP v. Kannan* was let off in exchange for his assistance. However, instead of reforming, he continued his match-fixing practices. He was prosecuted in *Rajendran s/o Kurusamy and Others v. Public Prosecutor* [1998] 2

132. *See* S/N 3 (the President) and S/N 5 (the committee member) of the FAS *List of Suspended Players/Officials for 2019 (Carried over to 2020), Suspended for Life*, https://www.fas.org.sg/wp-content/uploads/2020/01/List-of-Suspended-Players-and-Outstanding-Fines.pdf.pdf.

133. Football Association of Singapore (18 Mar. 2022), *FAS Lifts Ban on Kannan Kunjiraman and Thiru Rajamanickam*, https://www.fas.org.sg/fas-lifts-ban-kannan-kunjiraman-thiru-rajamanickam/ (accessed 22 Nov. 2023).

SLR(R) 814, along with his runner and the football team captain he had successfully bribed, in relation to the fixing of two local football matches. The trio were convicted after a trial. The Prosecution successfully appealed against the sentences for the three. The appellate court took into account the fact that the bookkeeper had continued his activities despite his brush with the law in *PP v. Kannan* and increased his sentence from six months' imprisonment to eighteen months' imprisonment. As for the football team captain, he was sentenced to a fine and ordered to pay a penalty at first instance. This was deemed manifestly inadequate by the appellate court,[134] which added an imprisonment term of two months to his sentence. In addition, he was given a lifetime ban from the sport by the FAS.[135] The runner's sentence of a fine and payment of a penalty was left untouched.

122. Other football players have faced penal sanctions for match-fixing activities. Mirko Jurilj[136] and Lutz Pfannenstiel[137] were each convicted under section 6 of the PCA and each was sentenced to five months' imprisonment for agreeing to influence the results of football matches. Mohamed Hakim[138] was convicted under section 6 of the PCA and sentenced to six months' imprisonment for accepting a bribe to get a red card during a football match, as well as offering another player a bribe to get a red card during the same match. All three were given lifetime bans by the FAS.[139]

123. Football coaches have not escaped punishment for match-fixing. A former Malaysian national coach was sentenced to a fine of SGD 50,000 for offering a bribe to a football player in a Singapore club to let goals in.[140]

124. Singapore's desire to combat match-fixing in order to boost its international reputation and its aspirations to be a sports hub has been reflected in the overall increase in severity of sentencing in recent years. For example, in 2014, the offender in *Public Prosecutor v. Ding Si Yang* [2014] SGDC 295 was sentenced to three years' imprisonment for supplying social escorts to provide sexual services to three match officials, in exchange for fixing football matches that the officials would be officiating. Upon the Prosecution's appeal, the sentence was increased in 2015 to

134. The appellate court noted that the team captain's behaviour was 'inexcusable' (para. 128) and noted that if the court was 'lenient to any particular footballer … it would send out a wrong message, not only to potential footballers playing in Singapore that we are not tough on football crimes, but also in setting a bad example to football fans for not preserving the name of the game in the spirit of sportsmanship' (para. 127).
135. *See* S/N 9 of the FAS *List of Suspended Players/Officials for 2017 (Carried over to 2018), Suspended for Life*, http://www.fas.org.sg/wp-content/uploads/2018/07/FAS-Midnight-Football-Challenge-2017-Suspensions-for-2018.pdf.
136. District Arrest Cases 36707 to 36709 of 2000 (unreported).
137. District Arrest Cases 36710 to 36712 of 2000 (unreported).
138. District Arrest Cases 2934 and 2935 of 2007 (unreported).
139. *See* S/N 12 (Mirko Jurilj), S/N 13 (Lutz Pfannenstiel), and S/N 14 (Mohamed Hakim) of the FAS *List of Banned Players/Officials* (correct as at 16 Mar. 2022), https://fas.org.sg/wp-content/uploads/2022/03/FAS-List-of-Banned-Players-Officials-correct-as-at-16-March-2022.pdf (accessed 22 Nov. 2023).
140. *Public Prosecutor v. Chow Kwai Lam*, District Arrest Case 31501 of 2006 (unreported).

five years' imprisonment. In 2018, the Prosecution launched an application to the Singapore High Court to realise assets that had been seized from the offender.[141]

125. The year 2015 saw a number of match-fixing convictions. In April, a former Malaysian football player pleaded guilty to conspiring with a Singaporean to bribe a Malaysian referee to fix the outcome of a match. The former football player was sentenced to two years' imprisonment.[142] The Singaporean, who pleaded guilty to a similar charge and to two cheating charges in October, was sentenced to an imprisonment term of thirty months.[143]

126. In addition, in July 2015, an Indonesia-registered football referee was convicted for conspiring with three other persons to bribe an official of the Timor Leste Football Association in exchange for the latter arranging for the Timor Leste football team to lose a match. The offender had previously received a ten-year ban from Indonesian football authorities for accepting bribes from various teams to influence the outcome of their matches. The offender was sentenced to thirty months' imprisonment.[144] One of his co-conspirators was the same bookmaker from *PP v. Kannan*, who evidently had not learnt his lesson despite the sentence of imprisonment he had received in 1998. He pleaded guilty to two charges under the PCA and was sentenced to forty-eight months' imprisonment. During the bookmaker's sentencing, the Prosecution called him 'Singapore's most prolific match-fixer in terms of convictions'.[145] The remaining two co-conspirators were given sentences of twenty months' and twenty-four months' imprisonment, respectively.[146]

127. Singapore has also gained notoriety from the alleged involvement of one Tan Seet Eng, commonly known as Dan Tan, in a global match-fixing ring. In November 2011, Italian authorities issued an arrest warrant for Tan as Tan was suspected of fixing 'dozens of games' in Italy and forwarded the warrant to the International Criminal Police Organization, more commonly known as INTERPOL.[147] The Italian investigations referred to Tan as 'Il Boss' and alleged that he directed and funded a network of European match-fixers from his home in Singapore.[148] In

141. Elaborated at para. 165, *infra*.
142. *Public Prosecutor v. Thanasegar S. Sinnaiah* (The Straits Times, 9 Apr. 2015), https://www.straitstimes.com/singapore/courts-crime/ex-malaysian-football-player-jailed-2-years-for-match-fixing (accessed 27 Jul. 2018).
143. *Public Prosecutor v. Selvarajan Letchuman* (The Straits Times, 10 Oct. 2015), https://www.straitstimes.com/singapore/courts-crime/30-months-jail-for-fixing-lionsxii-match (accessed 27 Jul. 2018).
144. *Public Prosecutor v. Nasiruddin* (The Straits Times, 22 Jul. 2015), https://www.straitstimes.com/singapore/jailed-for-bid-to-fix-football-match-at-sea-games (accessed 27 Jul. 2018).
145. Alkhatib, Shaffiq (24 Sep. 2015), *He was S'pore's most Prolific Fixer*, AsiaOne, https://www.asiaone.com/singapore/he-was-spores-most-prolific-fixer (accessed 27 Jul. 2018).
146. Chong, Elena (7 Nov. 2015), *Ex-football Manager Jailed for Match-Fixing*, The Straits Times, https://www.straitstimes.com/singapore/ex-football-manager-jailed-for-match-fixing (accessed 27 Jul. 2018).
147. Pianigiani, Gaia & Fuller, Thomas (13 Feb. 2013), *Soccer Fixing Inquiry Hinges on a Shadowy Singaporean*, The New York Times, https://www.nytimes.com/2013/02/14/sports/soccer/soccer-fixing-inquiry-focuses-on-tan-seet-eng-from-singapore.html (accessed 7 Aug. 2018).
148. Fisher, Jonah (5 Mar. 2013), *Trailing Singapore's 'Football Match-Fixing Boss'*, BBC News, https://www.bbc.com/news/world-asia-21653846 (accessed 7 Aug. 2018).

February 2013, INTERPOL's secretary general urged Singapore to move against Tan.[149] Tan was charged in absentia by a Hungarian court in May 2013 for his alleged role in match-fixing in Hungary.[150]

128. In September 2013, fourteen suspects, including Tan, were arrested on suspicion of being part of a global football match-fixing operation.[151] Shortly thereafter, in October 2013, Tan and three other persons[152] were detained in Singapore under Singapore's Criminal Law (Temporary Provisions) Act 1955 (hereinafter 'CLTPA'). Section 30 of the CLTPA provides that whenever the Minister of Home Affairs is satisfied that a person has been associated with activities of a criminal nature and that it is necessary for the person to be detained in the interests of public safety, peace and good order, the Minister may order that the person be detained for not more than twelve months from the date of the order. Pursuant to section 38 of the CLTPA, the President of Singapore may extend the validity of the order of detention for periods not exceeding twelve months at any one time.

129. The grounds of detention issued with Tan's detention order stated that between 2009 and 2013, Tan had been the leader and financer of a global football match-fixing syndicate operating from Singapore, which fixed football matches in many parts of the world.[153] Tan's detention order was renewed until a challenge brought by Tan succeeded in November 2015. Singapore's Court of Appeal ordered that Tan be released[154] on the basis that:

> 146 ... the grounds given for the detention set out few connections with Singapore. These are based on the Appellant's running of the syndicate from Singapore and his recruitment of runners in Singapore. While, as we have noted, these acts are reprehensible and should not be condoned, there is nothing to suggest whether (or how) these activities could be thought to have a bearing on the public safety, peace and good order within Singapore. The matches fixed, whether or not successfully, all took place beyond our shores. There is nothing in the grounds to indicate that the Appellant was working with overseas criminal syndicates or to suggest that such activities are likely to take root

149. The South China Morning Post (22 Feb. 2013), *Interpol Chief Urges Singapore to Arrest Match-Fixing Suspect Dan Tan*, https://www.scmp.com/sport/soccer/article/1155643/interpol-chief-urges-singapore-arrest-match-fixing-suspect-dan-tan (accessed 7 Aug. 2018).
150. The Straits Times (25 May 2013), *Singaporean Dan Tan Charged in Hungary Football Match-Fixing Probe*, https://www.straitstimes.com/world/singaporean-dan-tan-charged-in-hungary-football-match-fixing-probe (accessed 7 Aug. 2018).
151. The Straits Times (25 Nov. 2015), *From the Straits Times Archives: Who Is Dan Tan, the Singaporean Businessman and Alleged Match-Fixing Kingpin?*, https://www.straitstimes.com/singapore/courts-crime/from-the-straits-times-archives-who-is-dan-tan-the-singaporean-businessman (accessed 7 Aug. 2018).
152. Ministry of Home Affairs (2 Oct. 2013), *Detention Orders Issued on Four Persons for Being Part of Global Match-Fixing Syndicate*, https://www.mha.gov.sg/newsroom/press-release/news/detention-orders-issued-on-four-persons-for-being-part-of-global-match-fixing-syndicate (No Longer Available) (accessed 15 Aug. 2018).
153. *Tan Seet Eng v. Attorney-General and another matter* [2016] 1 SLR 779, at para. 8.
154. *Tan Seet Eng v. Attorney-General and another matter* [2016] 1 SLR 779.

in Singapore by reason of anything the Appellant has done or threatens to do. Nor is there anything to suggest that witnesses are being intimidated, resulting in their unwillingness to testify against the Appellant. We are thus unable to see how the grounds that have been put forward can be said to fall within the scope of the circumstances in which the power to detain under the CLTPA may be exercised by the Minister.

...

148 We therefore hold that the Appellant's detention was unlawful because it was beyond the scope of the power vested in the Minister, which was to detain persons in the circumstances where activities of a sufficiently serious criminal nature threatened to or did undermine public safety, peace or good order in Singapore.

130. The Minister of Home Affairs, however, was quick to react. Less than two weeks after Tan's release, a fresh detention order was issued in December 2015 against Tan for his suspected involvement in global football match-fixing activities. This fresh order 'expressly sets out the grounds which show the extent of Dan Tan's match-fixing activities from and within Singapore, and why this necessitates the issuance of a Detention Order under the CLTPA. The grounds set out the seriousness of Dan Tan's criminal activities over many years, their impact on public safety, peace and good order within Singapore, and the fact that he has intimidated witnesses to the extent that they continue to be unwilling to testify against him for fear of reprisal'.[155] Tan was eventually released in December 2019 on a Police Supervision Order.

131. In January 2016, it was reported that the three other persons who had been detained alongside Tan had been released from detention and were each placed under the less restrictive Police Supervision Order regime for the maximum three-year period.[156] Under a Police Supervision Order, a person is subject to several restrictions, including:[157]

- being required to reside within the limits of the police division stated in the Order;
- being required to inform the police officer in charge of the police division in which his residence is situated of his address;
- being not allowed to change his residence without written permission;
- being not allowed to leave Singapore without written permission;
- regular reporting to the police;
- curfew hours;

155. Ministry of Home Affairs (5 Dec. 2015), *MHA Statement on Detention of Dan Tan Seet Eng*, https://www.mha.gov.sg/mediaroom/press-releases/mha-statement-on-detention-of-dan-tan-seet-eng/ (accessed 7 Aug. 2018).

156. Ministry of Home Affairs (18 Jan. 2016), *MHA Statement on Three Members of Match-Fixing Syndicate Released from Detention and Placed on Police Supervision Orders*, https://www.mha.gov.sg/mediaroom/press-releases/mha-statement-on-three-members-of-match-fixing-syndicate-released-from-detention-and-placed-on-police-supervision-orders/ (accessed 15 Aug. 2018).

157. CLTPA, ss 33(1) and 34(1).

– electronic tagging; and/or
– not consorting with other persons who are subject to a Police Supervision Order.

132. Flouting these restrictions amounts to an offence, and the person is liable on conviction to imprisonment for a term between one and three years.[158]

133. One of the three persons who was released from detention in January 2016 was Gaye Alassane, who was a football player born in Mali, played for a football team in Singapore, and had been arrested with Tan in 2013. In 2003, he had been granted Singapore citizenship by virtue of his marrying a Singapore citizen. After his release from detention, the Ministry of Home Affairs served him with a Notice of Proposed Deprivation of Citizenship under Article 133(1) of the Constitution of the Republic of Singapore. Alassane referred his case to a citizenship committee, which recommended to the Minister of Home Affairs that he exercise his discretion and allow Alassane to retain his citizenship on compassionate grounds. The Minister then reconsidered his decision and decided to allow Alassane to retain his citizenship, subject to his conduct and behaviour.[159]

134. Tan's wife was also caught up in the proceedings against Tan. In June 2016, she was found guilty of lying to authorities about two of Tan's laptops, which she had tried to hide from the CPIB.[160] She was sentenced to two months' imprisonment, but this was subsequently reduced in November 2016 by the appellate court to three weeks' imprisonment, because no appreciable or potential harm had flowed from her action.[161]

135. Football is not the only sport to have suffered locally from the taint of match-fixing. In the first known case of e-sports match-fixing reported in Singapore, six professional e-sports players were handed bans by the tournament organiser Valorant Esports in June 2021.[162] The team captain had wagered that his team would lose zero-two to a rival team; this loss did subsequently occur. The captain had told four team members about his plan to lose, and tried to pay them off, but they had rejected him. These four team members were banned for six to twelve months from participating in Valorant competitions. The captain had obtained the money for his bets from a fellow competitive gamer who was not part of his team;

158. *Ibid.*, ss 33(3) and 34(2).
159. The Straits Times (7 Dec. 2017), *MHA to Strip Former S-League Player of Singapore Citizenship for Match Fixing*, https://www.straitstimes.com/singapore/mha-acts-to-strip-former-s-league-player-of-singapore-citizenship-for-match-fixing (accessed 7 Aug. 2018); and Ministry of Home Affairs (27 Jun. 2018), *Update on the Case of Deprivation of Citizenship*, https://www.mha.gov.sg/mediaroom/press-releases/update-on-the-case-of-deprivation-of-citizenship (accessed 7 Aug. 2018).
160. *Public Prosecutor v. Guan Enmei* [2016] SGDC 173.
161. Lum, Selina (16 Nov. 2016), *Jail Term for Ex-wife of Alleged Match-Fixer Dan Tan Reduced after Appeal*, The Straits Times, https://www.straitstimes.com/singapore/courts-crime/jail-term-for-ex-wife-of-alleged-matchfixer-reduced-after-appeal (accessed 7 Aug. 2018).
162. Sun, David (23 Jun. 2021), *S'pore professional gamers suspended for match-fixing, betting against own team in regional tournament*, The Straits Times, https://www.straitstimes.com/singapore/spore-professional-gamers-suspended-for-match-fixing-and-betting-against-own-team-in (accessed 24 Jun. 2021).

both players were banned from participating in Valorant competitions for three years. The captain was charged by prosecutors with corruption. He pleaded guilty and was sentenced to four months' imprisonment and ordered to pay a penalty of SGD 400.[163]

II. Other Corruption Offences

136. Corruption offences that do not involve match-fixing may also arise. For example, *Public Prosecutor v. Su Fengxian* [2018] SGDC 40 featured an accused person who had offered a bribe of EUR 2,000 to an STTA official to induce him to be lenient to her son, who was a member of the Singapore national team and who was facing disciplinary action for misconduct. During the trial, the accused person elected not to give any oral testimony. No other defence witness was called. The accused person was convicted and sentenced to a term of six weeks' imprisonment. She filed an appeal against conviction and sentence but eventually withdrew it.[164]

137. Following a vote-buying controversy, the then-Singapore Chess Federation President was banned in October 2015 from the World Chess Federation (hereinafter 'FIDE') for two years. He had allegedly agreed to secure a certain number of votes in support of one of the candidates running for the FIDE's presidency, in exchange for USD 500,000. Under the agreement, if the candidate won, the Singaporean would also head up an office to be set up by FIDE in Singapore.[165] No criminal sanctions have been brought against him for his alleged actions, but he was expelled with immediate effect from the Singapore Chess Federation's Executive Council.[166]

138. In February 2018,[167] it was reported that the President of a Singapore-based consultancy firm had been charged under section 182 of the Penal Code with giving false information to a CPIB officer, following investigations linked to a

163. Alkhatib, Shaffiq (26 May 2023), *Man Who Threw E-sports Valorant Match Gets 4 Months' Jail for Corruption*, The Straits Times, https://www.straitstimes.com/singapore/courts-crime/man-who-threw-e-sports-tournament-match-gets-4-months-jail-for-corruption (accessed 22 Nov. 2023).

164. Lum, Selina (5 May 2018), *Ex-national Paddler's Mum Starts Jail Term for Graft*, The Straits Times, https://www.straitstimes.com/singapore/courts-crime/ex-national-paddlers-mum-starts-jail-term-for-graft (accessed 15 Aug. 2018).

165. The Straits Times (28 Oct. 2015), *Singapore Ex-chess Official and Kasparov Get 2-Year Ban*, https://www.straitstimes.com/sport/singapore-ex-chess-official-and-kasparov-get-2-year-ban (accessed 15 Aug. 2018).

166. Singapore Chess Federation (28 Oct. 2015), *Changes to the SCF Executive Council*, https://www.singaporechess.org.sg/19-latest-news/401-changes-to-the-scf-executive-council (No Longer Available) (accessed 15 Aug. 2018).

167. Shaffiq Idris Alkhatib (15 Feb. 2018), *President of Singapore Company Linked to Olympic Probe Charged with Lying to CPIB Officer*, The Straits Times, https://www.straitstimes.com/singapore/courts-crime/president-of-singapore-company-linked-to-olympic-probe-charged-with-lying-to (accessed 17 Jan. 2019).

corruption and doping scandal in Russia. The Singapore firm had reportedly received monies from the Tokyo bid team to allegedly influence the vote to decide the 2020 Olympics host, as well as allegedly receiving monies from a Senegal company that were subsequently transferred to the spouse of a Russian athlete. The accused person had lied that his company had done legitimate work for the Senegal company and that he was tricked into making the subsequent transfer. He was sentenced to one week in jail.[168]

139. The Singapore High Court has also noted that there is no reason why a payment received by a sportsman from his employer cannot be corrupt. In *Sairi bin Sulaiman v. Public Prosecutor* [1995] 2 SLR(R) 794, the accused person was a jockey who had received a reward from a horse owner for riding the latter's horse to victory. He was convicted of corruption, and his appeal was dismissed. The Court noted that under the rules of the racing association that conducted the race, a jockey was entitled only to his riding fee and winning commission. He was not allowed to receive payments over and above what was permitted, without first seeking the racing association's consent. It did not matter that the ostensible purpose of the payment was for winning or doing one's best, instead of throwing the race. Such payments could put the recipient under a temptation to not do his best unless he received the gratification.

§6. Financial Offences

140. Various types of financial offences may occur in relation to sports, including criminal breach of trust (section 406 of the Penal Code), cheating (sections 417 and 420 of the Penal Code), forgery (section 465 of the Penal Code) and money laundering (section 47 of the CDSA).

141. Officials in sports bodies who have access to large amounts of funds may on occasion be tempted to dip into the pool for their own benefit. In 2002, the SSC uncovered irregularities in STBC's accounts, prompting an investigation by the Commercial Affairs Department of the Singapore Police Force. Having siphoned between SGD 1 million and SGD 2 million, the then-STBC President fled Singapore; he remains at large.[169] The investigations also uncovered that the then-general manager of STBC had made out cash cheques and withdrawn money that he handed to the STBC President to purchase computer and computer equipment. The STBC President had not purchased the equipment but had returned the money.

168. Lum, Selina (17 Jan. 2019), *Singaporean Linked to Major Russian Doping Scandal Jailed One Week for Lying to CPIB*, The Straits Times, https://www.straitstimes.com/singapore/courts-crime/singapore-man-linked-to-russian-doping-scandal-jailed-one-week-for-lying-to (accessed 17 Jan. 2019).

169. Siang Yee, Chua (15 May 2016), *Floorball Head in Alleged Fund Misuse*, The Straits Times, https://www.straitstimes.com/sport/floorball-head-in-alleged-fund-misuse (accessed 15 Aug. 2018).

Nevertheless, the general manager was charged in October 2003 with criminal breach of trust and falsification of accounts by making out fictitious payment vouchers. He was jailed for two months.[170]

142. In 2005, a finance executive from the Singapore Rugby Union allegedly embezzled SGD 1.2 million from the association and absconded.[171] He has yet to be located and to be dealt with by the authorities.

143. In 2006, a former national water polo team captain was given a nine-month imprisonment term for forgery and misappropriation of SGD 53,738 from the Singapore Swimming Association while he was its vice president.[172]

144. Also in 2006, a former Sports Executive at the Ceylon Sports Club pleaded guilty to one charge of criminal breach of trust, for misappropriating SGD 4,200 from the club. Given the relatively small amount involved, and the perpetrator's plea of guilt, lack of seniority in the club and lack of antecedents, he was sentenced to a fine of SGD 3,000.[173] An appeal was filed by the Public Prosecutor against the sentence; the outcome of the appeal is not reported.

145. In May 2016, SportSG filed a police report against the President of the Singapore Floorball Association on suspicion that he had misappropriated funds that belonged to the association.[174] He was charged in July 2018 with fourteen charges, including criminal breach of trust and forgery of cheques.[175] In November 2018, he pleaded guilty to three forgery charges and two criminal breach of trust charges, with the remaining charges being taken into consideration for sentencing purposes. He was sentenced to an imprisonment term of thirty months.[176]

146. Further to a receipt of a whistle-blowing letter, SportSG announced in April 2017 that it had filed a police report over suspected misuse of the funds of Tiong Bahru Football Club and a purported attempt by a senior official from Hougang United Football Club to obstruct the completion of audits of the Singapore Premier League's sit-out clubs. On the same day as the announcement, police conducted several raids

170. The Straits Times (17 Feb. 2004), *Ex-GM Jailed for Aiding in Funds Misuse* (accessible at National Library Board, Lee Kong Chian Reference Library, microfilm, reel number NL25510).
171. Osman, Shamir (21 Jun. 2017), *Former National Player Khoo Elected as Rugby President*, The New Paper, https://www.tnp.sg/sports/others/former-national-player-khoo-elected-rugby-president (accessed 15 Aug. 2018).
172. Siang Yee, Chua (15 May 2016), *Floorball Head in Alleged Fund Misuse*, The Straits Times, https://www.straitstimes.com/sport/floorball-head-in-alleged-fund-misuse (accessed 15 Aug. 2018).
173. *Public Prosecutor v. Yakge Oshan Buddhika Mendis* [2006] SGDC 101.
174. Siang Yee, Chua (15 May 2016), *Floorball Head in Alleged Fund Misuse*, The Straits Times, https://www.straitstimes.com/sport/floorball-head-in-alleged-fund-misuse (accessed 15 Aug. 2018).
175. Mohd Jamil, Ervina (27 Jul. 2018), *Bekas Presiden Persatuan Floorball Hadapi 14 Tuduhan, Termasuk Pecah Amanah*, Berita Harian, https://www.beritaharian.sg/setempat/bekas-presiden-persatuan-floorball-hadapi-14-tuduhan-termasuk-pecah-amanah (accessed 15 Aug. 2018).
176. Alkhatib, Shaffiq (3 Nov. 2018), *Ex-floorball Association Head Jailed for CBT and Forgery*, The Straits Times, https://www.straitstimes.com/singapore/courts-crime/ex-floorball-association-head-jailed-for-cbt-and-forgery (accessed 9 Nov. 2018).

and arrested four persons: the former President and general secretary of the FAS, and the chairman of the Hougang United club and his wife.[177] In September 2021, it was reported that no further action would be taken against the former President and general secretary of the FAS; no reason was given.[178] On 21 February 2023, four individuals were charged with offences relating to obstructing police investigations and forging the financial statements of two football clubs.[179]

147. In a separate matter, a former account and administrative assistant of the Hougang United Football Club was convicted and sentenced to two years' imprisonment for criminal breach of trust of sums totalling SGD 278,200. She had embezzled the monies from the club's safes over a period of less than two weeks.[180]

148. Those who wish to watch a sports event live may also become victims of financial scams. Online market platforms such as Carousell and Craigslist have led to an unregulated reseller's market burgeoning in Singapore. On occasion, buyers can fall prey to unscrupulous would-be sellers. It was reported that in 2018, the police received more than 200 reports of e-commerce scams involving the sale of concert and event tickets.[181] For example, in August 2018, it was reported that a scammer had allegedly cheated victims of at least SGD 2,000 by pretending that she wanted to sell tickets to a sold-out concert after breaking up with her boyfriend.[182] For one victim, it was agreed that the seller would provide a registered post tracking number, after which the victim would pay half the cost and the other half upon receipt of the tickets. The tracking number was provided, the victim paid half and subsequently realised that the tracking number was fake. Others paid the full cost but received envelopes with only a sheet of paper inside.

149. In October 2021, a former marketing and communications director with the Singapore Swimming Association was charged with cheating various persons after

177. Lin Fhoong, Low (20 Apr. 2017), *High Drama as Police Raid FAS Office, 3 Football Clubs*, Today, https://www.todayonline.com/singapore/police-raid-fas-3-football-clubs-police-report-lodged-against-tiong-bahru-fc (accessed 5 Mar. 2019).
178. Abdullah, Ahmad Zhaki (27 Sep. 2021), *No Charges Against Ex-FAS Senior Officials Zainudin Nordin, Winston Lee in Funds Misuse Probe: AGC*, Channel NewsAsia, https://www.channelnewsasia.com/singapore/no-charges-ex-fas-senior-officials-zainudin-nordin-winston-lee-funds-misuse-probe-agc-2204541 (accessed 22 Nov. 2023).
179. Singapore Police Force (21 Feb. 2023), *Four Persons Charged for Offences Relating to Obstructing Investigations and Forging the Financial Statements of Two Football Clubs*, https://www.police.gov.sg/Media-Room/News/20230221_4_prsn_chrg_fr_off_rltng_to_obstctg_invstgtns_n_frgng_the_fncal_statmnts_of_2_ftbll_clbs (accessed 23 Nov. 2023).
180. Lam, Lydia (30 Jul. 2019), *Hougang United Football Club Employee Jailed for Embezzling S$278,200*, Channel NewsAsia, https://www.channelnewsasia.com/news/singapore/hougang-united-football-club-employee-jailed-embezzling-11765680 (accessed 29 Mar. 2021).
181. Zhuo, Tee (17 Jan. 2019), *Over 200 Cases of Online Ticket Sale Scams Last Year*, The Straits Times, https://www.straitstimes.com/singapore/courts-crime/over-200-cases-of-online-ticket-sale-scams-last-year (accessed 17 Jan. 2019).
182. Sue-ann, Cheow (10 Aug. 2018), *Victims Pay Scammer for JJ Lin Concert Tickets but Get Sheets of Blank Paper Instead*, The Straits Times, https://www.straitstimes.com/singapore/courts-crime/victims-pay-scammer-for-jj-lin-concert-tickets-but-get-sheets-of-blank-paper (accessed 15 Aug. 2018).

receiving payment of about SGD 87,000 for football tickets, concert tickets, and shoes that he did not deliver.[183] He pleaded guilty and was sentenced to an imprisonment term of eighteen months.[184]

150. Another type of offence that may arise is one under section 54 of the CDSA, colloquially known as the 'money laundering' provision. The elements required to prove an offence under section 54 of the CDSA are: (i) the property in question represents benefits from criminal conduct; (ii) there is dealing by the accused person in that property, by way of concealment, disguise, conversion, transfer, removal out of jurisdiction, acquiring, possession or use; and (iii) the accused person knows that the criminal nature of the property that he is dealing with.[185] Hence, for example, if a person misappropriates monies from a sports body, and then uses it to buy a car, section 54 would have been breached.

§7. Harassment and Public Nuisance

151. A number of provisions criminalise acts of public nuisance. For example:

- Section 268 criminalises acts and omissions that constitute public nuisance and which cause any common injury, danger or annoyance to the public. This could include, for example, a person who urinates on the floor of a stadium. A perpetrator can be punished with a fine of up to SGD 1,000.
- If a sports fan sprays graffiti on a wall declaring his support for a particular sports team, that person would be liable under section 3 of the Vandalism Act (Cap 341) for vandalism and may be liable to a number of punishments, including a fine of up to SGD 2,000, imprisonment for up to three years, and/or caning of up to eight strokes.
- A spectator who has imbibed too much alcohol while watching a sports event may be liable under section 510 of the Penal Code for being drunk and disorderly if he 'cause[s] annoyance to any person' while in public. Such person can be punished with imprisonment of up to six months, or a fine of up to SGD 1,000, or both.
- Where a spectator shouts racist abuse at a football player during a game, the spectator could be open to criminal liability under section 4 of the Sedition Act (Cap 290) for promoting feelings of ill will and hostility between different races. Such offence is punishable with a fine of up to SGD 5,000, imprisonment of a term of up to three years or both. Alternatively, he could be prosecuted under section 298 of the Penal Code for uttering words with the deliberate intention of wounding

183. Tang, Louisa (2 Sep. 2021), *Ex-manager of Joseph Schooling's Swim School Charged with Cheating 21 People of over S$80,000*, Today, https://www.todayonline.com/singapore/ex-manager-joseph-schoolings-swim-school-charged-cheating-21-people-over-s80000 (accessed 29 Nov. 2023).
184. Lam, Lydia (20 Oct. 2021), *Ex-Singapore Swimming Association Marketing Director Gets Jail for Cheating Friends*, Channel NewsAsia, https://www.channelnewsasia.com/singapore/ex-singapore-swimming-association-mohamed-hafidz-jaafar-cheating-jail-2256347 (accessed 29 Nov. 2023).
185. *Public Prosecutor v. Ho Man Yuk and Others* [2017] SGDC 23, at para. 74.

the racial feelings of another person. The punishment for such act is imprisonment for up to three years or a fine, or both.

152. On a more individual front, the Protection from Harassment Act 2014 (hereinafter 'POHA') was enacted in 2015 to afford protection in the criminal and civil sphere against harassment and unlawful stalking. The POHA makes the following acts criminal:

(a) using threatening, abusive or insulting words or behaviour, with intent to cause harassment, alarm or distress to another person (section 3);
(b) using threatening, abusive or insulting words or behaviour which is heard, seen or otherwise perceived by another person likely to be caused harassment, alarm or distress (section 4);
(c) using threatening, abusive or insulting words or behaviour with intent to cause the victim to believe that unlawful violence will be used against the victim or any other person, or to provoke the use of unlawful violence by the victim or any other person (section 5); and
(d) unlawful stalking (section 7).

153. Examples where POHA could be invoked would include where an athlete is being stalked by an obsessed fan, where a spectator threatens a fellow spectator with bodily harm, or where vicious insults are traded between athletes.

§8. Restraint Orders and Seizure of Property

154. The authorities may seek to prohibit or prevent a person from dealing with property that is suspected to be the proceeds of or related to crime. The authorities may seize such property pursuant to section 35 of the CPC or may apply for a restraint order under section 16 of the CDSA.

I. Restraint Orders under the CDSA

155. Under section 19 of the CDSA, the Singapore High Court may make a restraint order to prohibit any person from dealing with any 'Realisable Property' (which is defined in section 2 to mean any property held by the defendant and gifts that are caught by the CDSA that have been made by the defendant to other persons).

156. A restraint order may only be made upon an ex parte application by the Public Prosecutor to a Judge in chambers and must provide for notice to be given to persons affected by the order.[186] A restraint order may only be issued by the Singapore High Court under the conditions listed in section 18(1) of the CDSA, namely where:

186. CDSA, s. 19(4).

(a) proceedings have been instituted against the defendant for a drug dealing offence or a serious offence;
(b) the proceedings have not been concluded; and
(c) the court is satisfied that there is reasonable cause to believe that the defendant has derived benefits from criminal conduct or drug dealing.

157. Property may be seized under the CDSA even if it does not form the traceable proceeds of an identifiable offence.[187]

158. Alternatively, pursuant to section 18(2) of the CDSA, the High Court may issue a restraint order if: (a) a person is informed that he may be prosecuted for a drug dealing offence or a serious offence or (b) that investigation for a drug dealing offence or a serious offence, as the case may be, has been commenced against a person who dies or cannot be found or is outside the jurisdiction.

159. The list of 'serious offences' is set out in the Second Schedule of the CDSA. It includes (but is not limited to) corruption, dishonest receipt of stolen property, criminal breach of trust, dealing in stolen property, cheating, forgery and money laundering.

160. Protective mechanisms in the CDSA expressly limit the imposition of a restraint order to prevent abuse. Section 19(5) states that a restraint order may be discharged or varied, and under section 19(6), property seized may be managed and dealt with in accordance with directions from the court.

161. If the Realisable Property is in the form of real property or securities, then the High Court may under section 20 of the CDSA make a charging order on the property to secure the payment to the Government of an amount equal to the value of the property charged. The conditions listed in section 18 also apply. Further, like a restraint order, the charging order may only be made upon an ex parte application by the Public Prosecutor to a Judge in chambers.[188]

II. Seizure under the CPC

162. Under section 35(1) of the CPC, the police may seize any property: (a) in respect of which an offence is suspected to have been committed; (b) which is suspected to have been used or intended to be used to commit an offence; or (c) which is suspected to constitute evidence of an offence.

163. If the property liable to be seized is held or suspected to be held in a financial institution, a police officer of or above the rank of an inspector may, by written

---

187. *Rajendar Prasad Rai and Another v. Public Prosecutor and Another Matter* [2017] 4 SLR 333, para. 58.
188. CDSA, s. 20(3).

order, (a) direct the financial institution to deliver the property to any police officer; or (b) direct the financial institution not to allow any dealings in respect of the property in such account or safe deposit box for a specified period.[189]

164. There is no express time limitation upon which a seizure order under section 35 of the CPC will be discharged. Instead, section 370(1) of the CPC requires that the law enforcement officer who seizes property under section 35 must make a report of the seizure to the court one year after the date of seizure.[190] Persons who would be affected by the disposal order (such as the person who is entitled to possession of the property, or who has a beneficial interest in the property) have a right to be heard.[191] The court will then decide whether or not to extend the seizure. If there is any pending court proceeding in relation to the property or if the court is satisfied that the property is relevant for the purposes of any investigation, enquiry, trial or other proceedings under any written law, then the property cannot be disposed of and will remain seized by law enforcement.[192]

165. In *Rajendar Prasad Rai and Another v. Public Prosecutor and Another Matter* [2017] 4 SLR 333, the Honourable the Chief Justice of Singapore sitting in his appellate capacity in the Singapore High Court held that in order for the court to extend the seizure, the court must be satisfied that the property was seized pursuant to the police's powers under section 35, and if so, that the property was reasonably believed to be the fruit or the traceable proceeds of an identifiable crime that the applicant was suspected to have committed.[193] The Prosecution would also ordinarily have to inform the court of the offence to which the seized property related, of the justification for the extension and of such other facts as formed the basis of its request.[194]

166. Where property has been seized under section 35 of the CPC, it will be disposed of pursuant to section 364 or 370 of the CPC. Procedures under section 364 of the CPC apply where property was seized and criminal proceedings took place. Where property was seized pursuant to investigations but no criminal proceedings followed, then the procedures under section 370 of the CPC apply.[195] If the property is no longer relevant for the purposes of any investigation, enquiry, trial or other proceedings, the court can make a suitable order in respect of the property. Thus, the court is empowered to order that the property be returned to its rightful owner(s) if it has not been shown to be traceable to an offence.

---

189. CPC, s. 35(2).
190. *Ibid.*, s. 370(1).
191. *Mustafa Ahunbay v. Public Prosecutor* [2015] 2 SLR 903, at para. 59.
192. CPC, s. 370(3).
193. *Rajendar Prasad Rai and Another v. Public Prosecutor and Another Matter* [2017] 4 SLR 333, para. 47.
194. *Ibid.*, paras 47 and 48.
195. *Sim Cheng Ho v. Lee Eng Soon* [1997] 3 SLR(R) 190.

§9. Confiscation Orders

167. In the event that a defendant is convicted of one or more serious offences in Singapore, the Public Prosecutor can apply for the court to make a confiscation order under section 6 of the CDSA against the defendant in respect of the benefits derived by him from criminal conduct.

168. A confiscation order will only be made after a reasonable opportunity has been given for persons holding any interest in the property to make representations to the court.[196] For example, if an option to purchase has been exercised by a bona fide third-party purchaser for a property that is caught within the confiscation order in exchange for valuable consideration, the purchaser may make representations to the court to prevent the property from being confiscated.

169. The court may assess the benefits that were derived from the criminal conduct and determine the amount to be confiscated. This amount is the amount that the court assesses to be the value of the benefits derived by the defendant from criminal conduct.[197]

170. For example, pursuant to the conviction of the offender in *Public Prosecutor v. Ding Si Yang* [2014] SGDC 295 for match-fixing, the authorities carried out a financial audit and determined that the offender's expenditure exceeded his known sources of income within the material period by about SGD 3.4 million. The authorities therefore applied for a confiscation order for the sum of SGD 3.4 million, which was granted by the Singapore High Court in May 2019.[198]

196. CDSA, s. 16.
197. *Ibid.*, s. 13.
198. Tan, Angela (9 May 2019), *Court Confiscates S$2.6m in Ill-Gotten Gains from Convicted Football Match-Fixer*, Business Times, https://www.businesstimes.com.sg/government-economy/court-confiscates-s26m-in-ill-gotten-gains-from-convicted-football-match-fixer (accessed 26 Mar. 2021).

Chapter 3. Sports and Tort Law

171. The difference between a crime and a tort is that the latter is a wrong done to society, whereas the former is a wrong done to an individual or particular individuals. Criminal prosecutions tend to be brought by the Public Prosecutor, although private prosecution may be commenced by one individual against another subject to a fiat being granted by the Public Prosecutor.[199] In contrast, tortious actions are generally brought by an individual or entity against another individual or entity.

172. The purpose of criminal prosecution and subsequent sentencing is multifold: deterrence, incapacitation, rehabilitation, retribution and restitution. On the other hand, tortious actions and the resulting damages are intended to protect a victim's rights and to compensate a victim for a wrong done. Nonetheless, the fact that the injuring party is forced to pay compensation can in a sense be viewed as punishment.

173. In relation to sports, tortious actions can take place in numerous situations. For example, if an athlete is injured during training or while participating in a sports event, a cause of action for tort of battery or tort of negligence may be made out. Spectators and referees may have a cause of action against the organiser or occupier of a sports venue in the event that the condition or safety of the venue is compromised. Persons who consume food served at a sports venue may have recourse via tortious claims in the event that the food is unhygienic and causes illness or disease. Residents who live near sports venues may be inconvenienced by events, such as balls flying out of a stadium, or even by noise or rowdy spectators, and may resort to claims of negligence or private nuisance.

174. Only a few sports-related tort cases have come before the Singapore courts. This chapter reviews the requirements to succeed in a tortious claim in Singapore and provides some case law examples. Where relevant, sports-related tort cases are referred to.

§1. Trespass to the Person

175. Athletes in sports competitions generally do not intend to inflict injury upon one another. However, accidents can occur. For example, in July 2009, a teenager participating in a taekwondo competition was kicked by his opponent in an otherwise routine bout. The teenager collapsed and died four days later from severe head injuries.[200] The State Coroner recorded a verdict of misadventure.[201]

199. CPC, s. 12.

200. Chong, Elena (18 Apr. 2010), *Head Kick Was 'Rather Light'*, The Straits Times, http://www.asiaone.com/News/Education/Story/A1Story20100416-210800.html (accessed 11 Oct. 2018).

201. *Misadventure Recorded in Teenager's Death During Taekwondo Tournament*, Channel NewsAsia (30 Apr. 2010).

176. Where, however, the injury is caused with intention, then the victim can bring an action for trespass to the person, which includes the torts of battery and assault. Trespass is actionable per se; i.e., the plaintiff is not required to prove damage. The plaintiff also does not need to show that the injury was reasonably foreseeable.

177. In *Amutha Valli d/o Krishnan v. Titular Superior of the Redemptorist Fathers in Singapore and others* [2009] 2 SLR(R) 1091, the Singapore High Court accepted the definitions of assault and battery as found in *Collins v. Wilcock* [1984] 1 WLR 1172 at 1177:

> An assault is an act which causes another person to apprehend the infliction of immediate, unlawful, force on his person; a battery is the action infliction of unlawful force on another person.

178. Assault therefore requires no more than a threat of force, whereas battery requires the actual application of force.

179. The elements of the torts of battery are: (a) direct physical contact with the plaintiff; (b) intentional physical contact with the plaintiff; and (c) unjustified physical contact.[202]

180. As for assault, the plaintiff must have reasonably apprehended actual physical contact at the time that the threat was made. This is an objective test based on what a reasonable person in the plaintiff's position would have known or been expected to know in the circumstances.[203] The plaintiff's apprehension must be in relation to an imminent battery, and not a threat of force in the future.[204]

181. In *Goel Adesh Kumar v. Resorts World at Sentosa Pte Ltd (SATS Security Services Pte Ltd, Third Party)* [2015] SGHC 289, the plaintiff visited the defendant casino and got into an argument with another patron. The casino's employees escorted the plaintiff to a side room to cool down and prevented him from leaving the room by physical means, including pushing him against the wall and restraining him by holding onto his arms. The plaintiff sued the casino for vicarious liability for tortious acts of false imprisonment, assault and battery by the casino's employees.

182. The Singapore High Court found that all three torts were made out. In relation to the tort of assault, the court held that the employees' actions had caused the plaintiff to reasonably apprehend the affliction of immediate, unlawful, force on him. Similarly, the actions of the employees in holding the plaintiff back, grabbing his arms and the scuffles that resulted in him being hit against the wall amounted to

---

202. Gary Chan Kok Yew, *The Law of Torts in Singapore* (Academy Publishing 2nd ed., 2016) (*The Law of Torts*), para. 02.015.
203. *The Law of Torts*, para. 02.030.
204. *Ibid.*, para. 02.033.

battery. The court found that such conduct was not conduct that is ordinarily acceptable in daily life and that the employees had not acted with lawful excuse (i.e., used reasonable force to prevent a breach of peace or in self-defence).

183. As to damages, the court noted that this 'involves a consideration of the degree of the tortfeasor's fault and the degree to which his acts contributed to the damage in question: *Downs and another v. Chappell and another* [1997] 1 WLR 426'. Regarding the false imprisonment claim, the court took into account the facts that the employees would not have sought to keep the plaintiff in the room if the plaintiff had not been rude or aggressive, that the room was comfortable and that the detention was for less than fifty minutes. Regarding the assault and battery claims, the plaintiff claimed that he had suffered a shoulder fracture, a labral tear, a rotator cuff injury and a frozen shoulder. The court considered the expert evidence and decided that the fracture was a result of the incident, but the other injuries were pre-existing. However, the court also noted that the incident considerably worsened the pre-existing injuries. A total sum of SGD 45,915.74 was awarded to the plaintiff.

§2. Negligence

184. Three elements must be established in order to succeed in an action for the tort of negligence:

(1) the existence of a duty of care owed by the defendant to the plaintiff;
(2) that the defendant has breached the duty of care owed to the plaintiff; and
(3) the defendant's breach caused the damage suffered by the plaintiff, and the damage suffered must not be too remote.

I. Duty of Care

185. In Singapore, the *locus classicus* on how to determine the existence of a duty of care is the Court of Appeal's judgment in *Spandeck Engineering (S) Pte Ltd v. Defence Science & Technology Agency* [2007] 4 SLR(R) 100 (*Spandeck*). In *Spandeck*, the appellant was awarded a contract by the Government of Singapore to redevelop a facility. The respondent was appointed as the superintending officer of the project and was responsible for certifying interim payments in respect of the appellant's work for the contract. The appellant claimed against the respondent for negligently undervaluing and under-certifying the appellant's work. On appeal, the threshold issue was whether there was a duty of care owed by the respondent to the appellant and the applicable test for ascertaining the existence of a duty of care.

186. The Court of Appeal held that the threshold question that the court must be satisfied is fulfilled (failing which the claim cannot take off)[205] is whether or not

205. *Spandeck*, para. 75.

there is factual foreseeability – was it foreseeable that the defendant's act might result in the harm that the plaintiff suffered?[206]

187. In *Ngiam Kong Seng v. Lim Chiew Hock* [2008] 3 SLR(R) 674, the appellants failed at this preliminary stage. The first appellant had been riding a motorcycle that was allegedly struck by the defendant's vehicle. Immediately after and during the period following the accident, the respondent represented himself to be a helpful bystander who had rendered assistance to the first appellant. The second appellant thus developed feelings of gratitude towards the respondent. She subsequently was told that the respondent had been involved in the accident. Thereafter, she suffered from major depression and suicidal tendencies resulting from having been 'betrayed' and claimed damages for the alleged psychiatric harm. The Court of Appeal held that '[t]o hold that it is reasonably foreseeable that the mere communication of the information in question without more could result in harm to a party boggles the imagination and stretches the realms of reality'.

188. If the threshold question of factual foreseeability is answered in the affirmative, the court then embarks on a two-stage framework comprising: (a) proximity and (b) policy considerations. The first stage of proximity requires sufficient legal proximity between the plaintiff and defendant.[207] The focus is on the closeness of the relationship between the parties themselves and involves physical proximity, circumstantial proximity (such as an overriding relationship of employer and employee or of a professional man and his client) and causal proximity (in the sense of the closeness or directness of the causal connection or relationship between the particular act or course of conduct and the loss or injury sustained).[208]

189. The first-stage test of proximity includes the twin criteria of voluntary assumption of responsibility and reliance, as essential factors in meeting the test of proximity. Where the plaintiff voluntarily assumes responsibility for his acts towards the defendant, and the defendant relies on it, it is only fair and just that the plaintiff be held liable for negligence in causing economic loss or physical damage to the defendant.[209]

190. If the threshold question of factual foreseeability is answered positively and the first stage of proximity is established, then a prima facie duty of care arises. Policy considerations are then applied to determine whether or not to negate the duty. Policy considerations include, for example, the presence of a contractual matrix which has clearly defined the rights and liabilities of the parties and the relative bargaining positions of the parties.[210]

---

206. *The Law of Torts*, para. 03.042.
207. *Spandeck*, para. 77.
208. *Ibid.*, para. 81 read with para. 78.
209. *Spandeck*, para. 81.
210. *Ibid.*, para. 83.

191. An example of where claims have failed at proving the existence of a duty of care lies in *Tomlinson v. Congleton Borough Council* [2003] 3 WLR 705. In that case, a lake was formed in a disused quarry in a park owned by the defendants. The defendants were aware that the lake attracted visitors in hot weather and made efforts to prohibit swimming by displaying notices that read 'dangerous water: no swimming' and employing rangers to give oral warnings against swimming and handing out safety leaflets. The plaintiff went into the lake, stood in shallow water, dived, struck his head on the bottom and broke his neck. He claimed damages against the defendants. The House of Lords ruled in the defendants' favour, holding that the plaintiff's injury had arisen not from the state of the defendants' premises, but rather from his own misjudgment in attempting to dive in too-shallow water. In paragraph 45, Lord Hoffmann had this to say:

> 45 I think it will be extremely rare for an occupier of land to be under a duty to prevent people from taking risks which are inherent in the activities they freely choose to undertake upon the land. If people want to climb mountains, go hang-gliding or swim or dive in ponds or lakes, that is their affair. Of course the landowner may for his own reasons wish to prohibit such activities. He may be think [sic] that they are a danger or inconvenience to himself or others. Or he may take a paternalist view and prefer people not to undertake risky activities on his land. He is entitled to impose such conditions, as the Council did by prohibiting swimming. But the law does not require him to do so.

192. A similar conclusion was reached by the English Court of Appeal in *Trustees of the Portsmouth Youth Activities Committee (A Charity) v. Poppleton* [2008] EWCA Civ 646. The applicant went for bouldering at the defendant's indoor climbing premises. The applicant was not an experienced climber. The wall rose up to a maximum height of 16 feet, and the floor was covered with shock-absorbent matting at least 12 inches thick. The applicant watched a friend leap off the wall and grab hold of a metal girder that crossed the room, before safely dropping to the floor. The applicant attempted the same manoeuvre but with the tragic ending of landing on his head on the matting and ending up tetraplegic. The court at first instance decided that the defendants were in breach of duty in failing to warn the applicant that thick safety matting did not make a climbing wall safe but might induce or encourage an unfounded belief that it did. This was unanimously overturned by the Court of Appeal. Lord Justice May stated:

> 20 There being inherent and obvious risks in the activity which Mr Poppleton was voluntarily undertaking, the law did not in my view require the appellants to prevent him from undertaking it, nor to train him or supervise him while he did it, or see that others did so. If the law required training or supervision in this case, it would equally be required for a multitude of other commonplace leisure activities which nevertheless carry with them a degree of obvious inherent risk – as for instance bathing in the sea ....

II. Breach of Duty

193. Once a duty of care has been established, the next consideration is whether the defendant has breached the duty on a balance of probabilities. As a preliminary step, in order to determine whether there has been a breach of duty, the standard of duty of care has to be established.

194. The standard of care is the objective standard of a reasonable person using ordinary care and skill.[211] There is nevertheless a subjective element, in that the standard changes depending on the circumstances. As stated by Sir John Donaldson MR in *Condon v. Basi* [1985] 1 WLR 855:

> The standard is objective, but objective in a different set of circumstances. Thus there will of course be a higher degree of care required of a player in a First Division football match than of a player in a local league football match.

195. As regards the standard of care owed by a participant in a game or competition to a spectator, the consensus in *Wooldridge v. Sumner* [1962] 3 WLR 616 was that a spectator 'takes the risk of any damage caused to him by any act of a participant done in the course of and for the purposes of the game or competition notwithstanding that such act may involve an error of judgment or a lapse of skill, unless the participant's conduct is such as to evince a reckless disregard of the spectator's safety'.

196. Furthermore, the standard of care is based on what was reasonably foreseeable as measured by the prevailing knowledge at the time of the event, and not after.[212]

197. Whether or not the duty of care owed by the defendant to the plaintiff was breached by the defendant will turn on the specific circumstances of each case.

198. In situations where the plaintiff is unable to explain the occurrence of the event by which he suffered damage,[213] he may rely on the doctrine of res ipsa loquitur. Erle CJ explained in *Scott v. The London and St Katherine Docks Company* (1865) 3 H & C that the doctrine applies where 'the thing is shown to be under the management of the defendant or his servants, and the accident is such as in the ordinary course of things does not happen if those who have the management use proper care'.[214]

199. The doctrine operates as a rule of evidence that an event which in the ordinary course of things is more likely than not to have been caused by negligence is by itself evidence of negligence. It would then be for the defendant to rebut the

211. *The Law of Torts*, para. 06.006.
212. *JSI Shipping (S) Pte Ltd v. Teofoongwonglcloong (a firm)* [2007] 4 SLR(R) 460, para. 69.
213. *Loh Siew Keng v. Seng Huat Construction Pte Ltd* [1998] SGHC 197, para. 240.
214. Quoted in *Teng Ah Kow v. Ho Sek Chiu* [1993] 3 SLR(R) 43, para. 23.

prima facie case.[215] For example, the defendant may offer an alternative explanation as to how the accident occurred, which does not involve his negligence.

200. The doctrine of res ipsa loquitur cannot be relied upon where the plaintiff makes a specific allegation as to the cause of the negligence but does not possess the evidence to prove his assertion.[216]

III. Causation and Remoteness of Damage

201. Finally, the plaintiff must prove that the damage was caused by the defendant and that the damage was not too remote.

202. For causation, two categories must be proved: causation in fact and causation in law. Causation of fact is commonly known as the 'but for' test, in that the plaintiff must prove that the damage to him would not have happened but for the defendant's negligent act. Where there is more than one cause in fact, the court will need to determine which factual cause is to be regarded as the cause for purposes of legal liability (i.e., causation in law).

203. In certain situations, a *novus actus interveniens* may break the chain of causation. An act or omission must be of such a nature as to constitute a wholly independent cause of the damage before the intervening conduct would be termed a *novus actus interveniens.*[217] For example, in *BNM v. National University of Singapore* [2014] 4 SLR 931, the deceased drowned in a swimming pool owned by the defendant. The High Court found that the lifeguards had been negligent in the discharge of their duties, but that causation was not proved because the medical evidence showed that the deceased had a heart condition and would not have survived even if the lifeguards had attended to him earlier. This result was upheld on appeal.

204. The plaintiff's own act may also serve to break the chain of causation, where his conduct is so 'reckless or deliberate',[218] or where his conduct is 'wholly unreasonable'.[219]

205. As for the remoteness rule, its purpose is to attribute legal liability only where the type of damage suffered by the plaintiff was reasonably foreseeable by the defendant at the time of the breach.[220] The defendant must also take the plaintiff as he finds him, with all of his pre-existing conditions (commonly known as the 'eggshell skull rule'). This includes the plaintiff's financial condition.

215. *Teng Ah Kow v. Ho Sek Chiu* [1993] 3 SLR(R) 43, para. 22.
216. *Sim Chiang Lee v. Lee Hock Chuan* [2003] 1 SLR(R) 122, para. 11.
217. *TV Media Pte Ltd v. De Cruz Andrea Heidi* [2004] 3 SLR(R) 543, para. 76.
218. *PlanAssure PAC v. Gaelic Inns Pte Ltd* [2007] 4 SLR(R) 513, para. 100.
219. *TV Media Pte Ltd v. De Cruz Andrea Heidi* [2004] 3 SLR(R) 543, para. 76.
220. *Saatchi & Saatchi Pte Ltd v. Tan Hun Ling* [2006] 1 SLR(R) 670, para. 11.

206. For example, in *Ho Soo Fong v. Standard Chartered Bank* [2007] 2 SLR(R) 181, the appellants approached the respondent to refinance three properties. The respondent agreed on the condition that the appellants settle pending court actions. The respondent lodged caveats against the three properties in the meantime. After more than a year, the appellants were still not allowed by the respondent to draw down on the loans. The appellants made multiple requests that the loan facilities be cancelled and the caveats withdrawn, but the respondent ignored all requests. In the meantime, a fourth property owned by the appellants was sold by another bank via a mortgagee's sale. The appellants brought an action against the respondent, arguing that the respondent's caveats on their three properties had prevented them from obtaining additional refinancing that would have enabled them to pay off the other bank to avoid the mortgagee sale.

207. The caveats had been lodged under section 128 of the Land Titles Act (Cap 157). Infringement of this provision is a statutory tort, and the Singapore Court of Appeal therefore applied tort principles in considering the case. Given that the respondent knew that the appellants were heavily indebted in respect of the fourth property and that the respondent had been repeatedly notified that the other bank would take action to recover the fourth property if the respondent's caveats continued to affect refinancing in respect of the three properties, it was held that the appellants' losses from the forced sale of the fourth property were reasonably foreseeable. The Court of Appeal also expressly overturned an earlier decision[221] in which it had relied on the English case of *Owners of Dredger Liesbosch v. Owners of Steamship Edison* [1933] AC 449 and held that a respondent could be liable for pecuniary loss suffered by a plaintiff if such loss is caused by the plaintiff's lack of financial resources.

IV. Defences

208. Where a plaintiff has succeeded in proving all elements necessary to sustain his action in negligence, the defendant may employ defences against his negligent conduct. Such defences are separate from arguments that the defendant may employ to rebut the plaintiff's prima facie claim in negligence (e.g., by arguing that the threshold question of factual foreseeability has not been answered affirmatively, or by citing a *novus actus interveniens* as breaking the chain of causation).

209. Defences that the defendant may raise include:

(a) *Ex turpi causa non oritur actio.*
(b) *Volenti non fit injuria.*
(c) Inevitable accident.
(d) Contributory negligence.

221. *Khushvinder Singh Chopra v. Mookka Pillai Rajagopal* [1999] 1 SLR(R) 130. In *Ho Sok Foong*, the Court of Appeal stated at para. 65 'that, in so far as *Khushvinder Singh* applied the *Liesbosch* principle, it should no longer be followed by a future court'.

210. The burden of proving the defence(s) raised lies on the defendant.

A. *Ex Turpi Causa Non Oritur* Actio

211. The maxim *ex turpi causa non oritur actio* is a principle of public policy and means that no court will lend its aid to a man who finds his cause of action upon an immoral or an illegal act.[222] This is because the court will not involve itself in a dispute between parties where both sides are equally tainted by the same wrong, with the defendant benefitting as a result.[223]

212. The doctrine is not confined to criminal wrongdoing but extends even to non-criminal conduct which carries the necessary degree of turpitude. 'Turpitude' encompasses all conduct, criminal or otherwise, which is capable of invoking the *ex turpi causa* doctrine.[224] This includes morally reprehensible or grossly immoral conduct.[225] It does not extend to statutory offences.[226] Examples of immoral conduct include procuring business by corruption[227] and conspiracy to deceive a third party by creating a sham share issue transaction.[228]

213. A material consideration is whether the plaintiff has to plead or rely on his own illegal conduct in order to find the claim.[229] There must be sufficient connection between the damage suffered by the plaintiff to the plaintiff's wrongdoing.[230] Furthermore, the damage that the defendant caused should be proportionate to the plaintiff's wrong – if the damage is excessive, then the defence would not be applicable.[231]

214. An example of where the *ex turpi causa* doctrine may apply would be a situation where the plaintiff and defendant agree to participate in high-speed street car racing with other parties, with the plaintiff getting into the defendant's car and the defendant driving, and the plaintiff then suffers injury due to a crash. The plaintiff's claim for damages against the defendant A similar situation arose in *Pitts v. Hunt* [1991] 1 QB 24, where the plaintiff was a pillion rider on a motorcycle driven by the deceased. The motorcycle was involved in a collision. The plaintiff and the deceased had been drinking prior to the incident, the plaintiff knew that the rider did not hold a driving licence and was uninsured, and at the time of the accident, the plaintiff was encouraging the rider to drive in a reckless and dangerous manner. The plaintiff brought an action in negligence against the defendant, who was the

222. Lord Mansfield CJ in *Holman v. Johnson* (1775) 1 Cowp 341 at 343.
223. *Ho Kang Peng v. Scintronix Corp Ltd* [2014] 3 SLR 329, para. 64.
224. *Ong Bee Chew v. Ong Shu Lin* [2017] SGHC 285, para. 131.
225. *United Project Consultants Pte Ltd v. Leong Kwok Onn* [2005] 4 SLR(R) 214, paras 54 and 57.
226. *Ibid.*, para. 57.
227. *Ong Bee Chew v. Ong Shu Lin* [2017] SGHC 285, para. 134.
228. *Koon Seng Construction Pte Ltd v. Chenab Contractor Pte Ltd* [2008] 1 SLR(R) 375, para. 72.
229. *Ibid.*, paras 35 to 38.
230. *The Law of Torts*, para. 08.012.
231. *Ibid.*

deceased rider's personal representative. The English Court of Appeal upheld the decision of the trial judge and dismissed the plaintiff's appeal.

215. In contrast, in *Rashid Osman bin Abdul Razak v. Abdul Muhaimin bin Khairuddin* [2013] 2 SLR 762, where a similar set of facts arose, the Singapore High Court granted judgment to the plaintiff because the plaintiff did not know that the motorcycle was stolen and that the defendant did not possess a valid motorcycle licence.

B. Volenti Non Fit Injuria

216. The defence of *volenti non fit injuria* (which is Latin for 'to one who is willing, no harm is done') is based on the plaintiff's consent to the risks of harm from the defendant's negligence. Three elements must be established for this defence:[232]

(1) the plaintiff's agreement to absolve the defendant from legal responsibility for the latter's conduct;
(2) the plaintiff's agreement was voluntary; and
(3) the plaintiff acted with full knowledge of the nature and extent of the risk of harm created by the defendant's negligence.

217. This defence is particularly relevant in the realm of sports activities, but its applicability ought to be differentiated from situations where no breach of duty has even taken place. In *Wooldridge v. Sumner* [1962] 3 WLR 616, a photographer was injured during a horse show when a horse galloped towards him; he took fright, stepped into the path of the horse and was knocked down. His reliance on the *volenti* defence was dismissed by the English Court of Appeal, with Lord Justice Diplock stating that 'any act of a participant done in the course of and for the purposes of the game or competition … involves no breach of the duty of care owed by the participant to him'.[233] The *volenti* defence was thus not applicable.

218. As another example, in *Blake v. Galloway* [2004] 1 WLR 2844, the plaintiff and defendant were with other friends. All were throwing twigs and pieces of bark at each other. The game was good-natured. The plaintiff threw a piece of park that struck the defendant on his body. The defendant picked up the bark and threw it back at the plaintiff; it struck his face and caused serious injury to his eye. At trial, the judge found for the plaintiff and rejected the defence that the plaintiff had consented to being struck. The decision was overturned on appeal. The English Court of Appeal found that the participants in the horseplay owed each other a duty to take reasonable care not to cause injury.[234] There would be a breach of duty only where

232. *The Law of Torts*, para. 08.024; Michael A. Jones, Anthony M Dugdale & Mark Simpson. *Clerk and Lindsell on Torts* (Sweet and Maxwell 21st ed., 2014), paras 3–95.
233. *Wooldridge v. Sumner* [1962] 3 WLR 616, at 634.
234. *Blake v. Galloway* [2004] 1 WLR 2844, para. 15.

conduct was reckless or at a very high degree of carelessness.[235] The conduct by the defendant was at its highest an error of judgment or lapse of skill and did not suffice to amount to a failure to take reasonable care in the circumstances of horseplay.[236]

219. The utility of the *volenti* defence can be negligible where a referee breaches the rules of the game. In *Smoldon v. Whitworth* [1996] EWCA Civ 1225, the plaintiff broke his neck while playing in a rugby match when a scrum collapsed. In his claim for damages, he argued that the referee's failure to apply and enforce the rules of engagement at the scrummage had led to a high number of scrums collapsing, including the scrum that led to his injury. The referee conceded that he owed a duty of care to the plaintiff. The English Court of Appeal held that one of the duties of a referee is to safeguard the safety of players and that the referee's failure to control the scrummage effectively amounted to a breach of his duty of care to the plaintiff.

220. *Vowles v. Evan* [2003] 1 WLR 1607 also featured a referee who breached the rules of the game. A front-row player in the plaintiff's rugby team went off injured. Under the rules of the game as issued by the Council of the International Rugby Football Board, the defendant referee was required to confer with the captain of the team to determine whether another player was suitably trained or experienced to take the place of the injured player, and if not, the game was to continue with non-contestable scrummages. The defendant conferred with the plaintiff's team captain and left it to the captain to make a decision. An inexperienced player was chosen; the defendant agreed without enquiring the player about his level of experience. Subsequently, a scrum did not engage properly and as a result, the plaintiff suffered permanent incomplete tetraplegia. The English Court of Appeal held that the defendant had breached his duty to exercise reasonable care for the safety of the players, by failing to satisfy himself that the replacement front-row player was suitably trained and experienced to play in the front row safely.

C. Inevitable Accident

221. A defendant who raises the defence of inevitable accident must prove that the event that caused harm to the plaintiff was purely accidental and was not deliberate or due to negligence.[237] The defendant must show that the event that happened could not have been prevented by the exercise of ordinary care, caution and skill.[238]

222. In *Loh Luan Choo Betsy v. Foo Wah Jek* [2005] 1 SLR(R) 64, the right rear tyre of a car driven by the defendant burst. Despite the defendant's efforts to brake and bring the car to a halt, the car went off the road. Its passengers, including the plaintiff, were injured. The defendant relied on the defence of inevitable accident.

235. *Ibid.*, para. 16.
236. *Ibid.*
237. *Saatchi & Saatchi Pte Ltd v. Tan Hun Ling* [2006] 1 SLR(R) 670, para. 5.
238. *Loh Luan Choo Betsy v. Foo Wah Jek* [2005] 1 SLR(R) 64, para. 28.

The Singapore High Court agreed that the defence was established. There was insufficient evidence to justify a holding that the defendant had not paid proper attention to his driving, that the defendant had not been driving at an excessive speed and that in braking, he had done his best to control the situation for the safety of everyone in the vehicle and with the exercise of ordinary care and skill.[239]

223. An analogy may be drawn in motor car sports. For example, if a race car's tyre bursts while it is racing on the track, causing the car to flip forward and into the spectator gallery and thereby causing injury to a spectator, the driver may be able to raise a defence of inevitable accident, in that he could not have prevented the car from somersaulting.

D. Contributory Negligence

224. Contributory negligence can be raised where there are at least two causes of the plaintiff's injury, and the plaintiff's conduct, act or omission was one of the causes. The defence of contributory negligence must be specifically pleaded and particulars in support thereof given.[240]

225. Section 3 of the Contributory Negligence and Personal Injuries Act 1953 makes it clear that where the damage caused is loss of life and/or personal injury, proof of the plaintiff's contributory negligence does not defeat the plaintiff's claim. Rather, the damages that are recoverable will be reduced to take into account the plaintiff's share in the responsibility for the damage.

226. Examples of where the partial defence of contributory negligence may be raised include where a motor car racing participant refuses to wear a helmet or flame-retardant gear, or where an American football player refuses to wear protective gear.

§3. Harassment

227. On 15 November 2014, the 'POHA' came into effect.[241] The purpose of the POHA is to protect persons against harassment and unlawful stalking by creating criminal offences of the same and by according civil remedies to victims.

228. The following are deemed offences under the POHA:

(a) intentionally causing harassment, alarm or distress by using threatening, abusive or insulting words or behaviour: section 3, POHA;

---

239. Paragraphs 31, 35, 43 and 44 of the judgment.
240. *Rajendran a/l Palany v. Dril-Quip Asia Pacific Pte Ltd* [2001] 1 SLR(R) 887, para. 19.
241. Protection from Harassment Act 2014 (Commencement) Notification 2014, s. 2.

(b) causing harassment, alarm or distress by using threatening, abusive or insulting words or behaviour: section 4, POHA;
(c) intentionally causing a victim to believe that unlawful violence will be done to him or any other person: section 5(1)(a)(i), POHA;
(d) intentionally provoking the use of unlawful violence by the victim or another person against any other person: section 5(1)(a)(ii), POHA;
(e) using any indecent, threatening, abusive or insulting words or behaviour towards a public servant in relation to the execution of the victim's duty as such public servant: section 6, POHA; and
(f) unlawful stalking: section 7, POHA.

229. Prior to the commencement of the POHA, the tort of harassment was a common law tort. This common law tort has been abolished pursuant to section 14 of the POHA. Today, harassment is a statutory tort under section 11 of the POHA, which allows a victim under section 3, 4, 5 or 7 of the POHA to bring civil proceedings against the perpetrator.

230. The victim may also apply for a protection order or an expedited protection order under sections 12 and 13 of the POHA respectively.

231. Section 17 of the POHA grants partial extraterritoriality to its provisions. As long as either the victim or perpetrator was in Singapore, the criminal and civil remedies for contravention of sections 3 to 7 are applicable.

232. An example in the sports context of the successful use of the POHA is found in the case of *Benber Dayao Yu v. Jacter Singh* [2017] 5 SLR 316. The appellant applied for a section 12 protection order in relation to a webpage posted on the Internet by the respondent. The webpage contained allegations that the appellant was an incompetent athletics coach who caused injuries to his trainees and that he molested the athletes whom he coached. The respondent's defence was that he had conducted himself reasonably in putting up the webpage. The Singapore High Court held that the respondent's actions were not reasonable; the webpage comprised personal attacks on the appellant, and there was no factual basis for the allegations made. The protection order was granted, ordering the respondent to remove the webpage and desist from publishing further insulting or abusive communications about the appellant. In addition, costs with reasonable disbursements were granted to the appellant.

233. The High Court also took the opportunity to set out the law in deciding whether to grant a protection order under section 12 of the POHA. The test comprises two stages: first, to establish whether the respondent has contravened the relevant provision of the POHA by examining the nature of the words or behaviour in question and, second, if the first stage is answered in the affirmative, to consider whether any defence can apply.[242]

---

242. *Benber Dayao Yu v. Jacter Singh* [2017] 5 SLR 316, para. 27.

234. The court must also consider whether it is just and equitable in all the circumstances to grant the protection order.[243] Factors include:[244]

(a) the nature and seriousness of the harassing conduct;
(b) the purpose and motive behind the conduct in question;
(c) the impact of the conduct on the victim and the degree of adverse emotional or psychological harm suffered;
(d) the degree to which the harassing conduct had been made known to the public;
(e) whether the victim had the means to mitigate or avoid the harassing conduct;
(f) whether the person behind the conduct had made genuine efforts to ensure that the conduct would not be misconstrued or misunderstood; and
(g) the ordinary instances of daily living that may be expected to be tolerated by reasonable persons.

§4. DEFAMATION

235. Sports athletes or officials may be the subject of defamatory words or publications. For example, in October 2017, an Australian cricketer successfully sued Fairfax Media for publishing articles that claimed he had indecently exposed himself to a masseuse. In November 2017, a former French minister was ordered to pay damages to tennis superstar Rafael Nadal after stating on a television show that his 2012 injury layoff was probably due to doping.

236. In Singapore, an action for the tort of defamation can be brought where the victim believes that his reputation has been maligned in some way.

237. To establish a prima facie case of defamation, three main legal requirements have to be fulfilled:

(1) the statement must refer to the plaintiff;
(2) the statement must be published; and
(3) the statement must be defamatory in nature.

238. A statement is defamatory in nature if it tends to:[245]

(a) lower the plaintiff in the estimation of right-thinking members of society generally;
(b) cause the plaintiff to be shunned or avoided; or
(c) expose the plaintiff to hatred, contempt or ridicule.

243. *Ibid.*
244. *Benber Dayao Yu v. Jacter Singh* [2017] 5 SLR 316, para. 54.
245. *The Law of Torts*, para. 12.015.

239. The meaning intended by the defendant is irrelevant for the purposes of determining what meaning the words complained of bear.[246] This is because the test as to whether a statement is defamatory is an objective one, by looking at the natural and ordinary meaning of the words and/or their innuendo meaning.[247] The defendant's state of mind is relevant only in relation to defences, such as fair comment, qualified privilege, consent and justification.

240. In ascertaining the 'plain and ordinary' meaning, the Court will determine 'what meaning the words would convey to an ordinary reasonable person, not unduly suspicious or avid for scandal, using his general knowledge and common sense'.[248] The words must be read objectively in the context of the whole publication while considering the manner and surrounding circumstances of the publication.[249]

241. If the plaintiff can establish that there were extrinsic facts that were known to readers of the words and that the knowledge of such extrinsic facts would cause a reasonable reader to understand the words to convey the defamatory imputation which went beyond or which altered their natural and ordinary meaning, then there is also defamation by innuendo. To establish this, the plaintiff bears the burden of proving that (a) there are facts extrinsic to the words, where such facts give rise to a defamatory imputation; (b) those facts were known to one or more of the persons to whom the words were published; and (c) knowledge of those extrinsic facts could cause the words to convey the defamatory imputation on which the plaintiff relies, to a reasonable person possessing knowledge of those extrinsic facts.[250]

242. To successfully invoke the defence of fair comment, the defendant must establish these four elements:[251]

(a) the words complained of are comments, though they may consist of or include inference[s] of facts;
(b) the comment is on a matter of public interest;
(c) the comment is based on facts; and
(d) the comment is one which a fair-minded person can honestly make on the facts proved.

243. The defence of qualified privilege accords a right to a person whose character or conduct has been attacked to answer such attack. Any defamatory statement he may make about the attacker will be privileged provided that the statement is published bona fide and is fairly relevant to the accusations made. The defence is

246. *Low Tuck Kwong v. Sukamto Sia* [2014] 1 SLR 639, para. 36.
247. *Goh Chok Tong v. Jeyaretnam Joshua Benjamin* [1998] 2 SLR(R) 971.
248. *Review Publishing Co Ltd and another v. Lee Hsien Loong and another appeal* [2010] 1 SLR 52, para. 27.
249. *Lim Eng Hock Peter v. Lin Jian Wei and another* [2009] 2 SLR(R) 1004, para. 91.
250. *Ibid.*, para. 106.
251. *Review Publishing Co Ltd and another v. Lee Hsien Loong and another appeal* [2010] 1 SLR 52, para. 139.

also available where the person who makes a communication has an interest or a duty (legal, social or moral) to make it to the person to whom it is made, and the person to whom it is made has a corresponding interest or duty to receive it.[252]

244. Categories of qualified privilege include:[253]

(a) statements made between parties who share a common or mutual interest in the subject of the communication;
(b) statements made in the discharge of a legal, social or moral duty;
(c) statements made in the protection of one's own self-interest; and
(d) fair and accurate reports of certain proceedings.

245. The defence of qualified privilege is defeated if the plaintiff can show that the defamatory statement was made with express malice.[254]

246. As for the defence of consent, proof of consent must be clear and unequivocal. The defendant must prove that the claimant has authorised or assented to the publication of the defamatory words complained of. The defence is to be narrowly construed: first, the defendant must prove that consent was given or can be adequately inferred with respect to each publication of defamatory material; and second, the defendant must prove that consent is clearly and unequivocally given to the fact of publication and to the content of the publication. It is not necessary for the plaintiff to have consented to the specific words found in the defamatory statements, but the court must give serious consideration to the scope of the plaintiff's consent.[255]

247. Where the defendant raises the defence of justification, he need only prove the sting of the charge. It is sufficient if the substance of the libellous statement be justified, and some leeway for exaggeration and error is granted.[256] The court need not 'engage in a meticulous examination of every word in question or every detail of fact'.[257] The defence would not be made out if a defendant's attempt to show that the defamatory statements are truly rested 'largely on unsubstantiated assertions of fact, tenuous circumstantial evidence and inferences'.[258]

248. The remedy for a tortious action of defamation is typically damages. An injunction may be granted, but only where it is clear that the statement complained

252. *Oei Hong Leong v. Ban Song Long David* [2005] 3 SLR(R) 608, para. 31.
253. *Lim Eng Hock Peter v. Lin Jian Wei and another* [2009] 2 SLR(R) 1004, para. 164.
254. *Ramesh s/o Krishnan v. AXA Life Insurance Singapore Pte Ltd* [2015] 4 SLR 1, para. 195.
255. *Ibid.*, paras 138–164.
256. *Chan Cheng Wah Bernard and others v. Koh Sin Chong Freddie and another appeal* [2012] 1 SLR 506, para. 44.
257. *Oei Hong Leong v. Ban Song Long David and others* [2005] 1 SLR(R) 277, para. 94.
258. *Arul Chandran v. Chew Chin Aik Victor* [2001] 1 SLR(R) 86, para. 37.

of was libellous and no defence could possibly apply,[259] or where the defendant persists in distributing the defamatory publication after the suit has commenced.[260] Declaratory relief is typically not granted, as it is generally given in Singapore only in respect of legal rights, and there is no legal right to good reputation.[261]

249. Furthermore, under section 15 of the POHA, a person who is the subject of a statement of fact that is false in particular about the person may apply to the Singapore courts for an order that no person shall publish or continue to publish the statement complained of unless that person publishes such notification as the court thinks necessary to bring attention to the falsehood and the true facts. Section 15 of the POHA can only be applied for by a natural person, and not by organisations or the Government of Singapore.[262]

250. Singapore has seen its share of sports-related defamation. In June 2017, a freelance writer published articles in relation to the stepping down of the chairman of a football club. The FAS filed a defamation suit against the writer. The case eventually settled, with the writer issuing a formal apology and the FAS agreeing that he could pay a nominal sum of SGD 4 in damages and costs.[263]

251. In December 2017, the President of the Singapore Gun Club was ordered to pay damages to the Singapore Rifle Association in relation to two defamatory statements that he had made about the latter.[264]

252. In September 2021, a defamation case involving two national marathoners was heard in Court.[265] During a South East Asian Games marathon event in 2015, some competitors missed a turn on the route. The plaintiff, who had taken the correct route, slowed down, thus enabling his competitors to catch up and resume the positions that they had held before the turn. The defendant, who won the event, later made several public social media posts alleging that the plaintiff had not slowed down. The trial judge *inter alia* held that (a) the statements were by their plain and ordinary meaning, and by innuendo, defamatory; and (b) the defences of justification and fair comment were not proved by the defendant. Damages of SGD 180,000, comprising SGD 120,000 in general damages and SGD 60,000 in aggravated damages, were awarded to the plaintiff. The decision was upheld on appeal.[266]

---

259. *Chin Bay Ching v. Merchant Ventures Pte Ltd* [2005] 3 SLR(R) 142, para. 37.
260. *Lee Hsien Loong v. Singapore Democratic Party* [2007] 1 SLR(R) 675.
261. *Low Tuck Kwong v. Sukamto Sia* [2014] 1 SLR 639, para. 122.
262. *Attorney-General v. Ting Choon Meng* [2017] 1 SLR 373.
263. The Straits Times (17 May 2018), *Football: Journalist Suresh Nair Sorry for Defamatory Articles, FAS Accepts Apology*, https://www.straitstimes.com/sport/football/football-journalist-suresh-nair-sorry-for-defamatory-articles-fas-accepts-apology (accessed 27 Nov. 2018).
264. Lum, Selina (4 Dec. 2017), *Singapore Rifle Association Wins Defamation Suit Against Singapore Gun Club President*, The Straits Times, https://www.straitstimes.com/singapore/singapore-rifle-association-wins-defamation-suit-against-singapore-gun-club-president (accessed 27 Nov. 2018).
265. *Liew Wei Yen Ashley v. Soh Rui Yong* [2021] SGDC 206.
266. Tham, Davina (28 Mar. 2022), *Runner Soh Rui Yong Fails in Appeal Against Defamation Suit Loss to Ashley Liew*, Channel NewsAsia, https://www.channelnewsasia.com/singapore/soh-rui-yong-ashley-liew-lose-appeal-defamation-high-court-2590621 (accessed 23 Nov. 2023).

253. In *Jasmin Nisban v. Chan Boon Siang and 20 Ors* [2023] SGDC 158, the plaintiff (who was formerly the Honorary Treasurer and elected Council member of the Singapore Chess Federation) won a defamation lawsuit against twenty-one defendants. A letter requisitioning an Extraordinary General Meeting had falsely alleged that the plaintiff was 'implicated' in an incident 'involving sexual misconduct'. Some of the requisitioners subsequently dissociated themselves from the defamatory statement, but the twenty-one defendants did not. The plaintiff hence commenced his suit. The Court, *inter alia,* held that (a) the statements were in their natural and ordinary meaning defamatory; (b) as the defendants failed to dissociate themselves from the statement, this amounted to retrospective assumption of responsibility from the publication of the statement; (c) defences of justification and fair comment were rejected; (d) the defence of qualified privilege was defeated as the plaintiff could prove that the defendants had acted with malice.

254. Apart from a civil action for defamation, the victim can file a police report alleging that section 499 of the Penal Code, which provides for the offence of criminal defamation, has been contravened. Section 499 arises where a person makes or publishes any imputation concerning any person, intending to or believing that the imputation will harm the reputation of such person. Certain exceptions apply, such as when the imputation is true and it is for the public good that the imputation be made or published. The punishment for a section 499 offence is an imprisonment term of not more than two years or fine, or both.

Chapter 4. Personality Rights

255. Broadly defined, the right of publicity is the right of an individual to control the use of his commercial identity. The right of publicity, also known as personality rights, is not expressly recognised in Singapore. The recourse for parties who wish to protect such rights is to resort to alternative causes of action, including protections afforded under the Personal Data Protection Act 2012 (hereinafter the 'PDPA'), as well as the tort of defamation and the tort of passing off.

§1. Personal Data Protection Act 2012

256. Section 3 of the PDPA makes it clear that the purpose of the PDPA is 'to govern the collection, use and disclosure of personal data by organisations'. 'Organisation' is widely defined to include 'any individual, company, association or body of persons, corporate or unincorporated'.[267]

257. Under section 13 of the PDPA, an organisation shall not collect, use or disclose an individual's personal data unless the individual has given or is deemed to have given consent to the collection, use or disclosure.

258. 'Consent' is granted where an organisation informs an individual of the purpose for the collection, use or disclosure of the personal data, on or before collecting the personal data, and the individual provides consent for that purpose.[268] Furthermore, an individual is deemed to consent to the collection, use or disclosure of his or her personal data by an organisation for a purpose if he or she voluntarily provides the personal data to the organisation for that purpose.[269]

259. 'Personal data' is defined as:[270]

> data, whether true or not, about an individual who can be identified –
>
> (a) from that data; or
> (b) from that data and other information to which the organisation has or is likely to have access;

260. The Advisory Guidelines on Key Concepts in the PDPA (revised on 16 May 2022) (hereinafter 'Advisory Guidelines') provides examples of certain types of data that are more likely to identify an individual:[271]

267. PDPA, s. 2(1).
268. *Ibid.*, s. 14 read with s. 20.
269. PDPA, s. 15.
270. *Ibid.*, s. 2(1).
271. Advisory Guidelines, para. 5.9.

- data that is assigned exclusively to an individual for the purposes of identifying the individual, such as passport number, or the National Registration Identity Card Number or Foreign Identification Number (all Singapore citizens and Singapore Permanent Residents are issued with the former, and all foreign nationals issued with immigration or work passes by Singapore's Ministry of Manpower are issued with the latter);
- data of a biological nature, such as facial image, fingerprint, iris print and finger-print.

261. An individual who believes that he has suffered loss or damage as a result of an organisation's contravention of the above-mentioned provisions of the PDPA is granted a right of action for relief in civil proceedings in court.[272] The court may grant relief by way of injunction or declaration, damages or such other relief as the court thinks fit.[273]

262. Therefore, where an athlete's image (which constitutes personal data) is used in an advertising campaign without his consent, the athlete could potentially seek recourse under the PDPA against the advertiser.

263. However, another exception granted by the PDPA is that an organisation may collect, use and disclose an individual's personal data without the individual's consent in certain situations that are specified in the First and Second Schedule of the PDPA.[274] This includes where the personal data is 'publicly available'.[275] Personal data is 'publicly available' where it is:

> generally available to the public, and includes personal data which can be observed by reasonably expected means at a location or an event –
>
> (a) at which the individual appears; and
> (b) that is open to the public.

264. In turn, the Advisory Guidelines state that personal data is 'generally available to the public' where 'any member of the public could obtain or access the data with few or no restrictions'.[276] An example is provided of a closed online social group with relatively open membership and which members of the public can join with minimal effort.[277] As for 'personal data which can be observed by reasonably expected means', this is an objective test.[278] Whether a location or event is 'open to the public' is determined by considerations such as the ease and ability with which

272. PDPA, s. 48O(1).
273. *Ibid.*, s. 48O(3).
274. *Ibid.*, s. 17.
275. *Ibid.*, First Schedule, Part 2, para. 1.
276. Advisory Guidelines, para. 12.85.
277. *Ibid.*, para. 12.86.
278. *Ibid.*, para. 12.90.

the public can gain access to the place.[279] The mere existence of restrictions such as entrance fees may not prevent the location from being regarded as open to the public.[280]

265. Given this, if an athlete's photograph is captured at an open sports event, and if that photograph is then used without his consent, the athlete's ability to seek redress under the PDPA would be limited.

266. Finally, the obligations under the PDPA do not apply to an individual acting in a personal or domestic capacity,[281] nor to an employee acting in the course of his employment with an organisation.[282] This is demonstrated by the following illustration provided by the Advisory Guidelines:[283]

> A travel agency collects personal data from Tom about his wife, Jane, when Tom books a travel package for a family holiday. Tom is not subject to the Data Protection Provisions as he is acting in a personal or domestic capacity. However, the travel agency must comply with all the Data Protection Provisions with regard to both Tom and Jane's personal data, unless one or more exceptions apply.

267. For example, if an athlete's fan persuades the athlete to take a 'selfie' photograph with the fan, and the fan then posts the photograph on online social media, then the athlete would be unlikely to find a remedy under the PDPA since the photograph was taken in the fan's personal capacity.

268. The use of the PDPA to uphold personality rights has yet to be tested. As noted by the Deputy Commissioner of the Personal Data Protection Commission in *In the matter of an investigation under section 50(1) of the Personal Data Protection Act 2012 v. My Digital Lock Pte. Ltd.* [2018] SGPDPC [3], at [50]:

> 50. Private individuals are likely to have more success in relying on the PDPA to prevent misuse or abuse of their identity on the basis of use or disclosure without consent. But these are not what the cases on publicity rights thus far deal with. Perhaps the PDPA and the right of publicity are means to different ends – while the right of publicity seeks to protect the commercial value of the name or image of the individual, the PDPA seeks to hold organisations accountable for the proper and respectful handling of personal data, by imposing a standard of conduct that permits reasonable use, processing or disclosure while preventing misuse or abuse of personal data. This distinction may, in

279. *Ibid.*, para. 12.91.
280. *Ibid.*, para. 12.92.
281. PDPA, s. 4(1)(a).
282. *Ibid.*, s. 4(1)(b).
283. Advisory Guidelines, para. 6.7.

future, guide the Commissioner's exercise of discretion when considering whether to commence investigations into complaints with personality rights undertones.

§2. TORT OF DEFAMATION

269. Before the advent of the PDPA, which came into effect on 2 July 2014,[284] two local cases featured the successful use of the tort of defamation as the cause of action in situations where photographs were used without consent.

270. In *Chiam See Tong v. Xin Zhang Jiang Restaurant Pte Ltd* [1995] 1 SLR(R) 856, the plaintiff was at the time a Member of Parliament. He and his party supporters had a birthday celebration at the defendant restaurant. A karaoke singing competition organised by the defendant to raise funds for charity was then in progress. The plaintiff was asked to sing, and his performance raised SGD 1,000. About a month later, the defendant published a newspaper advertisement that contained a photograph of the plaintiff holding a microphone. Next to his image was a caption in Chinese and a caption in English. The Chinese version stated that 'Member of Parliament Chiam See Tong's single song "Rong Shu Xia" raised $1,000.' However, the English version stated: 'Charity/Fund collection/Community Chest Activity Dedication Songs are welcome.' Two similar advertisements were also publicised in the form of handbills.

271. The Singapore High Court held that to the ordinary English reader who did not read Chinese, the use of the plaintiff's image suggested that he had consented to the use of his photograph for publicity either for gain or to sponsor a private restaurant and that he had done so by taking advantage of his position as a Member of Parliament. The court thus found that the newspaper and handbill advertisements were all defamatory of the plaintiff. The court further found that the defendant's purpose of using the plaintiff's photograph was to attract customers to the restaurant and had therefore wrongfully appropriated the plaintiff's reputation. An injunction was granted, and damages of SGD 50,000 were awarded to the plaintiff.

272. The second case is *Hanis Saini Hussey v. Integrated Information Pte Ltd (Lim Soo Boon t/a Tiffany Promotions, Third Party)* [1998] SGHC 219. The plaintiff was the first Singaporean model to achieve international success in the modelling industry and had made numerous appearances throughout her career in top international fashion magazines. The defendant was the sole proprietor of Tiffany Promotions, which was a social escort agency. The defendant published in the Singapore Yellow Pages an advertisement for the social escort agency, bearing a print of the plaintiff's image. The print had been commissioned by a society known as Action for AIDS in its campaign to promote AIDS awareness and had won many local and international advertising awards. After the publication of the agency's

284. Personal Data Protection Act 2012 (Commencement) Notification 2014, s. 2.

advertisement, the plaintiff received phone calls from her family and friends, asking about her 'new line of work' and how she was involved with the agency. The Singapore High Court held that:

> In view of the Plaintiff's high profile modelling career and the wide circulation of the print in connection with the Action for Aids campaign, the advertisement with the pictorial representation identical with the print would be identified with the Plaintiff by a sizeable section of the public if not at least by those in or connected with the modelling industry. I therefore held that the advertisement was defamatory of the Plaintiff.

273. Damages of SGD 30,000 were awarded to the plaintiff. An injunction was also granted to restrain the defendant from further publishing the print.

274. To date, there is no published decision involving the use of tort of defamation by an athlete in a suit for use of his/her image.

§3. Tort of Passing Off

275. The tort of passing off has not been used in Singapore to protect the commercial goodwill inherent in a celebrity's or athlete's identity. However, it has been successfully used in other jurisdictions, such as the United Kingdom[285] and Australia.[286]

276. Three elements must be established in order to succeed in a passing-off action: goodwill, misrepresentation and damage.[287]

277. In relation to goodwill, the classic description was propounded by Lord Macnaghten in *Commissioners of Inland Revenue v. Muller and Co Margarine* [1901] AC 217:

> What is goodwill? It is a thing very easy to describe, very difficult to define. It is the benefit and advantage of a good name, reputation, and connection of business. It is the attractive force which brings in custom. It is the one thing which distinguishes an old established business from a new business at its first start. The goodwill of a business must emanate from a particular centre or source. However widely extended or diffused its influence may be, goodwill is worth nothing unless it has a power of attraction sufficient to bring customers home to the source from which it emanates.

285. For example, *Irvine v. Talksport Ltd* [2002] 1 WLR 2355; *Fenty & Ors v. Arcadia Group Brands Ltd* (trading as Topshop) [2015] EWCA Civ 3.
286. For example, *Henderson v. Radio Corporation* (1960) 60 SR (NSW) 576; *Buttrose & Anor v. The Senior's Choice (Australia) Pty Ltd & Anor* [2013] FCCA 2050.
287. *Novelty Pte Ltd v. Amanresorts Ltd* [2009] 3 SLR(R) 216, at para. 37.

278. The Singapore Court of Appeal noted that goodwill is not in the mark, logo or get-up; it is the goodwill between a trader and his customers which is protected by this tort.[288] The court also distinguished between goodwill and reputation, holding that '[g]oodwill does not exist on its own and it attaches to a business. On the other hand, reputation may, and often does, exist without any supporting business'.[289]

279. Regarding misrepresentation, passing off requires that the defendant's action must have led or was likely to lead the public to believe that the goods or services offered by him are the goods or services of the plaintiff. Confusion is an essential element of the tort of passing off: although evidence of actual confusion is not required before a passing-off action can succeed, it is open to the court to infer a likelihood of confusion from the surrounding facts.[290]

280. Celebrity claims made in passing-off actions in other jurisdictions have typically asserted that the use of the celebrity's identifying features implied that: (a) the celebrity approved of the advertiser of the product, (b) the celebrity consented to the use of his or her identity by the advertiser or (c) there is some connection or association between the celebrity and the advertiser.[291]

281. Finally, a misrepresentation is not actionable unless it has caused, or is likely to cause, damage to the plaintiff's goodwill.[292] Examples of heads of damage are the injury to the plaintiff's reputation as a result of the misrepresentation that connected the plaintiff to the defendant, or if the defendant's misrepresentation exposed the plaintiff to legal liability or risk of litigation.[293]

---

288. *CDL Hotels International Ltd v. Pontiac Marina Pte Ltd* [1998] 1 SLR(R) 975, at para. 45.
289. *Ibid.*, at para. 46.
290. *Novelty Pte Ltd v. Amanresorts Ltd* [2009] 3 SLR(R) 216, at para. 77.
291. Tan, David. *The Celebrity Halo Effect and Passing Off*. Singapore Law Gazette, p. 15 (LexisNexis July 2017).
292. *Novelty Pte Ltd v. Amanresorts Ltd* [2009] 3 SLR(R) 216, at para. 94.
293. *The Law of Torts*, para. 14.108.

Part II. Sports and Employment

Chapter 1. Introduction

282. The professional athlete in Singapore is rare. Traditionally, most parents have placed emphasis on academic achievements in order to reap economic and career rewards. As a result, many athletes in Singapore juggle their sports activities with studies or a non-sports career.

283. Another potential obstacle to the focused pursuit of a professional sports career is National Service (hereinafter 'NS'). NS is the national requirement for all male Singapore citizens and permanent residents to undergo a period of mandatory service of approximately two years in the uniformed services (namely, the Singapore Armed Forces, the Singapore Police Force, or the Singapore Civil Defence Force). Typically, a person subject to the NS requirement is required to register for NS around the age of 18. Deferment of registration for NS is possible but is not often granted. A typical reason given for a deferment request is for further studies, but deferment is not granted for degree courses regardless of whether the applicant's studies have begun.[294] In a decision presided over by the Honourable Chief Justice of Singapore, the Singapore High Court sitting in its appellate capacity noted that '[w]hen a person refuses to serve NS at the time that he is required to and instead returns to serve at a time of his own choosing, or worse, at an age when he can no longer serve, his actions strike at the very core of the principles of national security, universality and equity'.[295]

284. Therefore, 'to preserve equity for all national servicemen, [Singapore's Ministry of Defence] will only defer individuals very selectively if their deferment serves Singapore's interest first and foremost, never their own. That is the only basis'.[296]

285. In relation to sports, deferment of NS is 'granted only to those who represent Singapore in international competitions like the Olympic Games and are

294. Central Manpower Base, *Deferment Cut-Off Age for Further Studies*, https://www.cmpb.gov.sg/web/portal/cmpb/home/before-ns/pre-enlistment-process/deferment-for-studies (accessed 19 Dec. 2018).

295. *Public Prosecutor v. Sakthikanesh s/o Chidambaram and other appeals and another matter* [2017] 5 SLR 707, at para. 48.

296. Mr Ng Eng Hen (6 Aug. 2018), *Singapore Parliamentary Report vol. 94*, sitting no. 81, available at https://sprs.parl.gov.sg/search/#/sprs3topic?reportid=oral-answer-48 (accessed 19 Feb. 2018).

potential medal winners for Singapore'.[297] Only three athletes – Joseph Schooling, Quah Zheng Wen and Maximilian Soh – have met these criteria between 2003 and 2018.[298] In 2018, a teenage footballer who had signed a professional contract with the English football team Fulham Football Club applied for deferment of his NS. When the teenager's father was asked when the teenager intended to return to Singapore to serve NS, he did not commit to a date and expressed that the teenager's professional career would be put first. The deferment application was thus rejected by the Ministry of Defence, which deemed that the teenager's 'actions are meant to further his own professional career, not national interest'.[299] It was subsequently reported that the teenager failed to report for NS when required to do so and that he has been deemed to have defaulted on his NS obligations.[300]

286. Deferment of NS has also been granted to e-sports players who represent Singapore in international competitions. In 2005, an e-sports player was granted a three-month deferment of NS, reportedly to allow him to participate in the Singapore finals of the World Cyber Games.[301] More recently, in August 2019, another e-sports player was granted a four-month deferment of NS; the deferment allowed him to participate as a member of the Singapore team in the Overwatch World Cup tournament in the United States of America.[302] Subsequently, the Ministry of Defence clarified that the basis of the deferment was for the individual to enrol for a vocational education course, as opposed to participation in the tournament.[303]

287. With the Government's support of sports culture, there has been increasing acceptance of the pursuit of a sports career. For example, the Singapore Sports School was officially opened on 2 April 2004. It is the only school in Singapore that offers its students an integrated academic and sports programme and has produced

---

297. MINDEF (16 Jul. 2018), *Reply to ST Query on Benjamin Davis' Request for Long-Term Deferment from Full-Time NS*, https://www.mindef.gov.sg/web/portal/mindef/news-and-events/latest-releases/article-detail/2018/july/16jul18_mq (accessed 19 Dec. 2018).
298. Osman, Shamir (16 Jul. 2018), *No NS Deferment for Fulham Teen Ben Davis: Mindef*, The Straits Times, https://www.straitstimes.com/sport/tennis/no-ns-deferment-for-davis-mindef (accessed 19 Dec. 2018).
299. MINDEF (18 Jul. 2018), *Reply to Media Queries on the Rejection of Benjamin Davis' Deferment from Full-Time NS*, https://www.mindef.gov.sg/web/portal/mindef/news-and-events/latest-releases/article-detail/2018/july/18jul18_mq (accessed 19 Dec. 2018).
300. Today (18 Feb. 2019), *Footballer Ben Davis Has Defaulted on NS Obligations: MINDEF*, https://www.todayonline.com/singapore/footballer-ben-davis-has-defaulted-ns-obligations-mindef (accessed 19 Feb. 2019).
301. Mr Tan Soo Khoon (16 Jan. 2006), *Singapore Parliamentary Report vol. 80,* sitting no. 15, available at https://sprs.parl.gov.sg/search/#/topic?reportid=020_20060116_S0005_T0001 (accessed 29 Mar. 2021).
302. Huang, Bryan (6 Aug. 2019), *Singapore Esports Player Granted NS Deferment, Will Play in Overwatch World Cup*, https://sg.news.yahoo.com/singapore-esports-player-granted-ns-deferment-will-play-in-overwatch-world-cup-095531827.html (accessed 29 Mar. 2021).
303. MINDEF (7 Aug. 2019), *Reply to Media Queries on Figo 'Azalea' Chua*, https://www.mindef.gov.sg/web/portal/mindef/news-and-events/latest-releases/article-detail/2019/August/07aug19_mq (accessed 29 Mar. 2021).

Olympian athletes. Student-athletes are given further opportunities through programmes such as the through-train programme and the School-within-a-School programme. The through-train programme allows selected student-athletes to skip the Singapore-Cambridge General Certificate of Education Ordinary Level examination and to proceed directly with the International Baccalaureate Diploma Programme, or a diploma programme with a local polytechnic.[304] The School-within-a-School programme allows selected student-athletes to work their academic programmes around their competition and training regime.[305] For example, a typical class size holds a maximum of twenty-five student-athletes, but the School-within-a-School class size is limited to not more than five student-athletes, providing them with greater attention from teachers. The students can keep up with their studies over electronic learning platforms while overseas and are given make-up lessons when they return to Singapore.[306]

288. In terms of funding, athletes are given financial support in the tiered Sports Excellence Carding system (hereinafter 'spexCarding').[307] In turn, spexCarding comes under SportSG's High Performance Sports system. Each NSA can nominate Singapore citizens, Singapore Permanent Residents, or Foreign Sports Talents who are Employment Pass holders, for spexCarding. SportSG will consider the athlete's performance over the past twelve months, as well as the athlete's potential to achieve at major games and world-level events (such as the Olympic Games, the Paralympic Games, the International Association of Athletics Federations World Championships, the Commonwealth Games, the Asian Games, the Asian Paralympic Games and the Southeast Asian Games). The amount of financial support given to the athlete depends on the level of carding to which the athlete is assigned. All spexCarded athletes are further given a training assistance grant (the value being determined by their carding level). Athletes at all levels are given access to sports medicine services and a sports medical insurance policy. A grant of up to SGD 3,000 per month for loss of wages is also provided to spexCarded athletes who opt to train full-time for up to twelve months in preparation for a major game.

289. An enhanced level of financial support is also given via the Sports Excellence Potential programme (hereinafter 'spexPotential') and the spexScholarship programmes.[308] The spexPotential programme provides support to athletes to enable them to achieve gold medal success at the level of the South East Asian Games, within a time-bounded period, with the long-term aim of transitioning the athlete

---

304. Singapore Sports School (undated), *Post-Secondary Programmes*, https://www.sportsschool.edu.sg/academics/post-secondary-programmes (accessed 22 Nov. 2023).
305. *Singapore Sports Guide 2015/2016* (Marshall 10th ed. Cavendish 2015), p. 20.
306. Singapore Sports School (undated), *A 'School' Within Singapore Sports School*, https://www.sportsschool.edu.sg/news-and-publications/archive/jul11/a-school-within-singapore-sports-school (accessed 18 Jan. 2019).
307. Details may be viewed at https://www.sportsingapore.gov.sg/files/Our%20Work/Singapore%20Sports%20Institute/High%20Performance%20Planning/2024singapore%20high%20performance%20sports%20handbook%20version10%20.pdf (accessed 23 Nov. 2023).
308. *Ibid.*

into the spexScholarship programme. The spexScholarship programme aims to prepare athletes to excel at major games at the Asian and World levels. Each NSA can nominate Singapore citizens for the spexPotential and spexScholarship programmes. Eligibility criteria include the athlete's track record, being able to demonstrate potential for further development, being able to commit to the demands of a full-time training load, attitude and behaviour, and being in medal contention for major games and world-level events. Athletes under the spexPotential and spexScholarship programmes are given a monthly stipend, financial support to cover the costs of coaching, training, competition and equipment, and education, career and personal development support. As at April 2021, the spexScholarship had been awarded to seventy-six recipients across twenty sports and six para-sports.[309]

290. Efforts have also been made to develop Singapore's athletes holistically in the areas of education, career and life skills, via the spexEducation[310] and the spexCareer. Both share the aim of implementing a comprehensive athlete support system designed to help athletes achieve their academic aspirations without compromising their pursuit of sports excellence.

291. Under spexEducation, student-athletes gain preferential admission into schools[311] by virtue of their sports achievements, are permitted alternative arrangements for examinations, are allowed to take multiple leaves of absence from school and so on. Student-athletes are also provided with education counselling and support letters for admission or scholarship applications.

292. spexCareer is operationalised through the Sports Excellence Business Network (hereinafter 'spexBusiness') for athletes. Employers from diverse industries offer career development support in the form of internships, apprenticeships, job placements and flexible workplace practices (such as allowing part-time work arrangements, flexi-leave, compression of the workweek into fewer days, provision of flexi-place arrangements and so on). As at November 2023, sixty-two business partners had joined the spexBusiness network.[312] As at December 2020, a total of 314 athletes had been placed with spexBusiness partners.[313]

309. spexBusiness eNewsletter Issue 14 (April 2021), https://www.sportsingapore.gov.sg/files/Our%20Work/Singapore%20Sports%20Institute/Athlete%20Life/SpexBusiness/spexBusiness_eNewsletter_emPOWER_issue_14.pdf (accessed 23 Nov. 2023).

310. Details may be viewed at https://www.sportsingapore.gov.sg/singapore-sport-institute/athlete-life/spexeducation/ (accessed 23 Nov. 2023).

311. As of November 2023, seventeen institutes are partners with spexEducation, including local universities and polytechnics (*see* https://www.sportsingapore.gov.sg/singapore-sport-institute/athlete-life/spexeducation/).

312. https://www.sportsingapore.gov.sg/spexbusiness-network-partners/ (accessed 23 Nov. 2023).

313. spexBusiness eNewsletter Issue 13 (December 2020), https://www.sportsingapore.gov.sg/files/Our%20Work/Singapore%20Sports%20Institute/Athlete%20Life/SpexBusiness/spexBusiness_eNewsletter_emPOWER_issue_13.pdf (accessed 23 Nov. 2023).

Chapter 2. Sources of Employment Law

293. There is no specific legislation in Singapore that governs the employment contracts of professional athletes. Rather, the Employment Act 1968 is the main labour law that governs employment in Singapore. The Employment Act is supplemented by other legislation such as the Employment of Foreign Manpower Act 1990 (hereinafter the 'EFMA'), the Central Provident Fund Act 1953 and the Workplace Health and Safety Act 2006.

294. Substantial amendments have been made to the Employment Act with effect from 1 April 2019.[314] These amendments are across three key areas:

(1) Core provisions (relating to, e.g., minimum days of annual leave, paid public holiday entitlement, sick leave entitlement, timely payment of salary and protection against wrongful dismissal) have been extended to cover all managers and executives. These core provisions were previously enjoyed only by manual workers, office employees and managers and executives whose basic monthly salary does not exceed SGD 4,500.
(2) Part 4 of the Employment Act (which provides additional protection in areas relating to, e.g., rest days, hours of work, annual leave, retrenchment benefit and retirement benefit) has been extended to cover more employees. The Part 4 protections were previously enjoyed by manual workers whose basic monthly salary does not exceed SGD 4,500 and other employees whose basic monthly salary does not exceed SGD 2,500. With effect from 1 April 2019, these protections were extended to employees whose basic monthly salary does not exceed SGD 2,600. Manual workers whose basic monthly salary does not exceed SGD 4,500 continue to enjoy the Part 4 protections.
(3) Enhancement of the employment dispute resolution framework. Previously, wrongful dismissal claims were dealt with by the Ministry of Manpower, whereas the Employment Claims Tribunal dealt with salary-related disputes. With effect from 1 April 2019, both types of claims are being dealt with by the Employment Claims Tribunal, in order to provide a 'one-stop service'. On 1 April 2019, the Ministry of Manpower, National Trades Union Congress, and the Singapore National Employers Federation jointly published the Tripartite Guidelines on Wrongful Dismissal, which contain illustrations of wrongful dismissal, such as for reasons of discrimination, deprivation of benefits, desire to punish an employee for exercising an employment right and for providing a false reason for dismissal. They also include examples of dismissals that are not wrongful, such as dismissals on grounds of poor performance, misconduct, and redundancy.[315]

---

314. Mrs Josephine Teo (20 Nov. 2018), *Singapore Parliamentary Report vol. 94*, sitting no. 86, available at https://sprs.parl.gov.sg/search/#/sprs3topic?reportid=bill-335 (accessed 27 Feb. 2019).
315. Ministry of Manpower (1 Apr. 2019), https://www.mom.gov.sg/newsroom/press-releases/2019/0401-tripartite-partners-release-guidelines-on-what-constitutes-wrongful-dismissal (accessed 29 Mar. 2021).

295. There is currently no legislation in Singapore that prohibits regulations in the constitutions of sports bodies or international sports associations from being incorporated into employment agreements with athletes. For example, a professional football player in Singapore is subject to the terms of his employment contract with his football club, as well as the FIFA Regulations on the Status and Transfer of Players (hereinafter 'RSTP'). Where either the player or the team does not abide by the obligations set out in the RSTP, then a claim could be made by the injured party to FIFA for compensation on the basis that the RSTP has been breached.[316]

§1. Core Provisions of the Employment Act

296. The salary period can be agreed upon between employer and employee but cannot exceed one month.[317]

297. Salary must be paid before the expiry of the seventh day after the last day of the salary period.[318] Additional payments for overtime work must be paid not later than fourteen days after the last day of the salary period during which the overtime work was performed.[319]

298. If an employee has been dismissed, then his salary must be paid not later than within three days of the date of dismissal.[320]

299. If employment is terminated by the employee, then his salary must be paid on the day on which his employment ends if due notice was given.[321] If the employee terminates his employment without notice or before the expiry of the notice period, then salary must be paid before the expiry of the seventh day after the day he terminates his employment.[322]

300. Only authorised deductions can be made from salary such as deductions for absence from work, damage to goods, loss of goods, accommodation supplied by the employer and meals supplied by the employer at the employee's request.[323]

301. Mandatory minimum periods of notice for termination of employment are set out in the Employment Act, as follows:[324]

(a) one day's notice for employment for a period less than twenty-six weeks;

---

316. Article 22, RSTP (March 2022 edition).
317. Employment Act, s. 20(2).
318. *Ibid.*, s. 21(1).
319. *Ibid.*, s. 21(2).
320. *Ibid.*, s. 22.
321. *Ibid.*, s. 23(1).
322. *Ibid.*, s. 23(2).
323. *Ibid.*, ss 26 to 30.
324. *Ibid.*, s. 10(3).

(b) one week's notice for employment for a period of at least twenty-six weeks and less than two years;
(c) two weeks' notice for employment for a period of at least two years and less than five years; and
(d) four weeks' notice for employment for a period of at least five years.

302. The length of notice must be the same for both employer and employee.[325]

303. Notice need not be given if the terminating party pays the other party a sum equal to the amount of salary that would have accrued to the employee during the notice period.[326] Notice is not needed for termination in the event of wilful breach by the other party of a condition of the employment contract,[327] or in the event of misconduct inconsistent with the fulfilment of the express or implied conditions of his service.[328]

304. An employment contract is deemed to be broken by an employer if he fails to pay salary according to the provisions of the Employment Act.[329] An employment contract is deemed to be broken by an employee if he is absent from work for more than two days continuously without reasonable excuse, or by not informing and not attempting to inform the employer of the excuse for the absence.[330]

305. Unless otherwise stated in the employment contract, the party who breaks the employment contract is liable to pay to the other party a sum equal to the amount of salary that would have accrued to the employee during the notice period.[331]

306. The Employment Act also sets out a number of provisions to prevent abuse of manual labourers, the majority of which are foreigners. Provisions include that salaries must be paid in legal tender[332] and that the employer cannot stipulate how the employee may spend his salary.[333]

307. All employees are granted minimum days of sick leave as long as the employee has worked for the employer for at least three months. The minimum number of days of sick leave depends on the length of time that the employee has served the employer and ranges from five to fourteen days per year.[334]

308. Regardless of nationality, all female employees are granted twelve weeks of maternity leave, as long as the employee has worked for the employer for at least

325. *Ibid.*, s. 10(2).
326. *Ibid.*, s. 11(1).
327. *Ibid.*, s. 11(2).
328. *Ibid.*, s. 14(1).
329. *Ibid.*, s. 13(1).
330. *Ibid.*, s. 13(2).
331. *Ibid.*, s. 16.
332. *Ibid.*, s. 54.
333. *Ibid.*, s. 55.
334. *Ibid.*, s. 89.

three months prior to the day of confinement.[335] If the child born is a Singapore citizen, the maternity leave is for a period of sixteen weeks.[336] The employee cannot be given notice of dismissal during her absence, or on such a day that the notice will expire during her absence.[337] Fathers whose children are born Singapore citizens or whose children become Singapore citizens within twelve months of the birth are granted up to four weeks of paternity leave if the child is born on or after 1 January 2024 (where a child is born before 1 January 2024, the paternity leave entitlement is two weeks).[338] Employees who are mothers or fathers are granted two days of childcare leave each year as long as the employee has worked for the employer for at least three months, and the child is less than 7 years old.[339]

309. Pursuant to section 8 of the Employment Act, any contract of service that provides a condition of service that is less favourable to an employee than any of the conditions of service prescribed by the Act is illegal, null and void to the extent that it is so less favourable.

§2. Part 4 of the Employment Act

310. The additional protections accorded by Part IV of the Employment Act include the following:

- provision of one rest day per week, or for an employee engaged in shift work, a continuous period of thirty hours;[340]
- no employee can be required to work more than six consecutive hours;[341] and
- no employee can be required to work more than eight hours in one day, or more than forty-four hours in one week.[342]

311. The limit in hours may be exceeded in certain situations, including accidents, work that is essential to the life of the community, work essential for defence or security, urgent work to machinery or plant or an interruption of work that is impossible to foresee.[343]

335. *Ibid.*, s. 76.
336. Child Development Co-Savings Act 2001, s. 9.
337. Employment Act, s. 81.
338. Child Development Co-Savings Act 2001, s. 12H.
339. Employment Act, s. 87A(1).
340. *Ibid.*, s. 36.
341. *Ibid.*, s. 38(1)(a).
342. *Ibid.*, s. 38(1)(b).
343. *Ibid.*, s. 38(2).

Chapter 3. Foreign Athletes

312. Foreign professional athletes may be employed in Singapore, subject to the possession of a valid work pass. A foreign athlete who is employed under a contract of service and who fails to obtain the requisite work pass is guilty of an offence and shall be liable on conviction to a fine, or imprisonment, or both.[344] His employer would also be guilty of an offence.[345] Furthermore, a foreign employee cannot work outside the scope and period specified in the work pass.[346] To do so amounts to an offence punishable by fine.[347]

313. The issuance of work passes is determined by Singapore's Ministry of Manpower. Failure by employers to abide by employment laws can result in work pass privileges being revoked. For example, in October 2018, the Ministry of Manpower barred a local football club from hiring foreign athletes pursuant to the club's failure to pay salaries on time. The suspension was lifted only after the club made rectifications on payments owed.[348] The same restriction was imposed in May 2019 when salaries were again not paid. In November 2019, the club was charged with 107 counts of not paying salaries on time.[349] On 11 January 2022, the club was fined SGD 26,000 after pleading guilty to seven charges, with another 127 charges taken into consideration for sentencing purposes.[350] In total, the club had failed to pay more than SGD 300,000 in salaries to thirty-five employees, including players and the coach. The club has since made restitution in full to its employees.

314. Those who enter Singapore under a visit pass are not allowed to work at all.[351] Those who enter Singapore under a dependant's pass may work only if he/she obtains a letter of consent issued by the Controller of Work Passes under the EFMA.[352]

315. Each sport may also have its own rules regarding the employment of foreign athletes. For example, the FAS sets down a limit on the number of foreign players (under which Singapore Permanent Residents are categorised) that can be signed by a Singapore Premier League team. The maximum number for the 2020 season

344. Section 5(7), EFMA.
345. Section 5(6), EFMA.
346. Sections 5(3) and 12, EFMA.
347. Section 5(7A), EFMA.
348. Sazali Abdul Aziz (22 May 2019), *Football: Warriors Banned from Hiring Foreign Personnel*, The Straits Times, https://www.straitstimes.com/sport/football/warriors-banned-from-hiring-foreign-personnel (accessed 29 Mar. 2021).
349. Sazali Abdul Aziz (8 Nov. 2019), *Warriors FC Charged with 107 Counts of Not Paying Employees' Salaries*, The New Paper, https://www.tnp.sg/news/singapore/warriors-fc-charged-107-counts-not-paying-employees-salaries (accessed 29 Mar. 2021).
350. Lam, Lydia (11 Jan. 2022), *Warriors Football Club Fined S$26,000 for Failing to Pay Player Salaries and Other Offences*, Channel NewsAsia, https://www.channelnewsasia.com/singapore/warriors-football-club-fined-s26000-failing-pay-player-salaries-and-other-offences-2427301 (accessed 23 Nov. 2023).
351. Immigration Regulations, Regulation 12(7).
352. *Ibid.*, Regulation 11(9).

was four (up from three in 2019), with an age restriction on one of the four players.[353] The age restriction was removed with effect from the 2021 season.[354]

§1. Foreign Sports Talent Scheme

316. Singapore has welcomed foreign athletes to become naturalised citizens through the Foreign Sports Talent Scheme (hereinafter 'FSTS'). The FSTS was first launched in 1993 under the name of Project Rainbow. The scheme has been used to attract foreign talent to represent Singapore at sports events, as it provides a fast track to Singapore citizenship. As stated by the then-Minister for Community Development during a speech in January 2000, 'Foreign sports talents are imported not only to win medals for Singapore but also for the purpose of interaction and sparring with our local athletes to partner, challenge and motivate the latter to excel.'[355]

317. The principles for the FSTS are threefold: openness to global talent, fairness in treatment between local and foreign-born athletes and integration into the Singapore way of life.[356] The latter is implemented by the NSA responsible for bringing in foreign talent and can include homestays with locals, visits to cultural and historical sites, language classes and learning to sing the Singapore National Anthem;[357] and attending National Day events, visiting schools and performing community service.[358] The foreign talents are also assigned local mentors to facilitate their integration.[359] The NSA is further obliged to comply with other conditions, such as having an education plan for younger foreign talents and post-sports career planning for the athletes.[360]

353. Football Association of Singapore (22 Nov. 2019), *Key Developments Implemented for Singapore Premier League 2020 Season*, http://www.fas.org.sg/key-developments-singapore-premier-league-2020-season/ (accessed 29 Mar. 2021).
354. Football Association of Singapore, *Singapore Premier League Regulations*, https://www.fas.org.sg/wp-content/uploads/2021/05/2021-Singapore-Premier-League-Competition-Regulations.pdf; https://fas.org.sg/wp-content/uploads/2022/08/AIA-Singapore-Premier-League-2022-Regulations-caa-130222.pdf; https://fas.org.sg/wp-content/uploads/2023/02/Singapore-Premier-League-2023-Regulations-CAA-23-February-2023.pdf (accessed 23 Nov. 2023).
355. Mr Abdullah Tarmugi (15 Jan. 2000), *Keynote Address at Sports 21 @ SSC at the Grassroots Club*, https://www.nas.gov.sg/archivesonline/data/pdfdoc/2000011502.htm (accessed 19 Dec. 2018).
356. Mr Teo Ser Luck (9 Mar. 2007), *Singapore Parliamentary Report vol. 82,* col. 3479, available at https://sprs.parl.gov.sg/search/#/topic?reportid=005_20070309_S0004_T0001 (accessed 19 Dec. 2018).
357. *Ibid.*
358. Mr Lawrence Wong (6 Feb. 2013), *Singapore Parliamentary Report,* vol. 90, sitting no. 4, available at https://sprs.parl.gov.sg/search/#/sprs3topic?reportid=oral-answer-540 (accessed 19 Dec. 2018).
359. *Ibid.*
360. Associate Professor Dr Yaacob Ibrahim (16 Mar. 2004), *Singapore Parliamentary Report,* vol. 77, col. 2050, available at https://sprs.parl.gov.sg/search/#/topic?reportid=004_20040316_S0003_T0003 (accessed 19 Dec. 2018).

318. As at the year 2000, preference was accorded to the sports deemed as 'Core' and 'Merit' sports that wished to bring in foreign sports talent. Younger athletes, belonging to an individual rather than a team sport, were also preferred.[361] Over time, however, this perception changed. As of November 2009, foreign sports talents numbered thirty-nine persons, comprising 4.6% of the 845 athletes in seven key sports,[362] including the team sport of football.[363] As of February 2013,[364] sixty-four athletes have been granted citizenship under the FSTS and have represented Singapore in thirteen sports.[365]

319. The contributions of foreign sports talents to Singapore's medal pool are evident. At the 2007 Southeast Asian Games, foreign talents accounted for 34.9% of the gold medals, even though they only formed 7.6% of the entire contingent.[366] In the 2012 Olympics, the two medals won by Singapore were by athletes brought in under the FSTS.

320. The achievements of foreign sports talents are also recognised in that they tend to be in the higher spexCarding levels and therefore receive more financial support. As of March 2008, 23.8% of the total amount spent by SportSG on direct athlete support grants went towards support for foreign talents, although they comprised 5.6% of the total number of carded athletes.[367]

---

361. Mr Abdullah Tarmugi (15 Jan. 2000), *Keynote Address at Sports 21 @ SSC at the Grassroots Club*, https://www.nas.gov.sg/archivesonline/data/pdfdoc/2000011502.htm (accessed 19 Dec. 2018).
362. Namely, athletics, badminton, bowling, football, swimming/water polo, table tennis and sailing.
363. Dr Vivian Balakrishnan (23 Nov. 2009), *Singapore Parliamentary Report,* vol. 86, col. 1811, available at https://sprs.parl.gov.sg/search/#/topic?reportid=048_20091123_S0009_T0002 (accessed 19 Dec. 2018).
364. Mr Lawrence Wong (25 Feb. 2013), *Singapore Parliamentary Report,* vol. 90, sitting no. 7, available at https://sprs.parl.gov.sg/search/#/sprs3topic?reportid=written-answer-1275 (accessed 19 Dec. 2018).
365. Namely, athletics, badminton, basketball, chess, cue-sports, fencing, football, hockey, netball, shooting, swimming, table tennis and water polo.
366. Mr Teo Ser Luck (5 Mar. 2008), *Singapore Parliamentary Report*, vol. 84, col. 2225, available at https://sprs.parl.gov.sg/search/#/topic?reportid=004_20080305_S0003_T0002 (accessed 19 Dec. 2018).
367. *Ibid.*

Chapter 4. Social Security

321. The Central Provident Fund (hereinafter 'CPF') is the social security system for Singapore citizens and permanent residents to set aside funds chiefly for retirement. The funds may also be used for property ownership, healthcare and asset enhancement.

322. Each CPF member holds three accounts up to the age of 55: an Ordinary Account, a Special Account and a MediSave account. The Ordinary Account can be used to pay for housing, insurance, education and investment. The Special Account cannot be utilised until the age of 55, but its interest rate is higher than that of the Ordinary Account. The MediSave account can only be used to pay for medical and dental fees (including hospitalisation, surgery, outpatient treatment and rehabilitative care).

323. For Singapore citizens and permanent residents who are under a contract of service to an employer, the employer is obliged to make contributions to the employee's CPF accounts.[368] The employer may recover a certain fraction of the contribution amount from the employee. Section 27(1)(h) of the Employment Act allows an employer to make deductions from an employee's salary in order to recover the aforementioned fraction of the contribution amount.

324. Where an employee is aged 55 or below, his employer's contribution to his CPF account is 37% of his total wages, of which 20% can be recovered from the employee's wages. The percentages increasingly reduce as the employee ages: at its lowest, when the employee is aged above 65, his employer's contribution to his CPF account is 12.5% of his total wages, of which 5% can be recovered from the employee's wages.

325. Professional athletes who sign contracts with a team or employer are liable to make CPF contributions, as they would be deemed employees. The stipend that is paid to athletes who receive the spexScholarship is not subject to CPF because the stipend is a training allowance.[369]

326. Self-employed persons (e.g., freelance coaches) must make CPF contributions to their MediSave account.[370] Self-employed persons are required to register with the CPF Board when commencing business. The First Schedule of the Central Provident Fund (Self-Employed Persons) Regulations sets out the rates payable.

---

368. CPF Act 1953, s. 7(1).
369. SportSG, Singapore High Performance Sports Handbook (version 9.3 dated 19 Sep. 2022), p. 23, query 11, accessible at https://www.sportsingapore.gov.sg/files/Our%20Work/Singapore%20Sports%20Institute/High%20Performance%20Planning/Singapore_High_Performance_Sports_Handbook_2021-V92_19Sep2022.pdf (accessed 23 Nov. 2023).
370. CPF Act 1953, s. 13A(1) read with the Central Provident Fund (Self-Employed Persons) Regulations.

327. Failure to make CPF contributions is an offence.[371] The offender is liable on conviction to a fine of not less than SGD 1,000 and not more than SGD 5,000, or imprisonment for a term not exceeding six months, or both.[372]

328. Foreigners do not have a CPF account, and therefore they and their employers need not make any CPF contributions.

329. During the CPF member's lifetime, he can choose to nominate person(s) to whom the funds in his CPF accounts will be paid upon his death.[373] If no nomination is made, then the total amount in the deceased's CPF accounts will be paid out to the Public Trustee in accordance with the Intestate Succession Act 1967 (or under section 112 of the Administration of Muslim Law Act 1966, if the member was a Muslim at the time of his death).[374]

371. CPF Act 1953, s. 58(b).
372. *Ibid.*, s. 61(2).
373. *Ibid.*, s. 25(1).
374. *Ibid.*, s. 25(2).

Chapter 5. Taxation

§1. Personal Income Tax

330. Generally, all income earned in or derived from Singapore is chargeable to income tax. Income may come from sources such as employment; carrying on a trade, business, profession or vocation; property; investments; lottery winnings; and so on.

331. Singapore uses a progressive tax rate, where higher-income earners are taxed at a higher rate than lower-income earners. Annual income of not more than SGD 20,000 is not taxable; any sum above the initial SGD 20,000 is taxable at a rate ranging between 2% and 24% with effect from the Year of Assessment 2024.

332. Tax liability for foreigners depends on tax residency status. A foreigner is regarded as a tax resident if (a) he stays or works in Singapore for at least 183 days in a year, or (b) he stays or works in Singapore continuously for three consecutive years, or (c) he is employed for at least 183 days for a continuous period over two years. A foreign tax resident will be taxed on all income earned in Singapore at the progressive resident rate but can enjoy tax relief. A foreign non-tax resident will be taxed on all income earned in Singapore at a specified flat rate or the progressive resident rate (whichever results in a higher tax amount) and is not entitled to tax relief.

333. Professional athletes, whether foreign or local, will be taxed on all income earned from employment, including sports awards and any payment derived from sports activities (e.g., prize money, sponsorship fees, endorsement fees, spexCarding stipends).[375]

334. Student-athletes who study full time and do not have income other than the spexScholarship or other sports awards would not be subject to income tax, as they are not deemed to be earning from any 'trade, business, profession or vocation' or 'employment'.[376]

335. Where a person has a full-time non-sports career, but takes part in sports competitions from which he receives sports awards, he is not subject to income tax on the sports awards, as he is not earning from any 'trade, business, profession or vocation' or 'employment' in relation to his sports ability.

§2. Withholding Tax

336. Where a person makes payment of a certain nature to a non-resident company or individual, the payer is required to withhold a percentage of that payment

375. Inland Revenue Authority of Singapore, *Essential Tax Information for Sportspersons Who Received Sports Awards for Representing Singapore*, https://www.iras.gov.sg/media/docs/default-source/uploadedfiles/pdf/faqs-for-sportspersons.pdf?sfvrsn=59ac7efb_7 (accessed 23 Nov. 2023).
376. Section 10(1), Income Tax Act 1947.

and pay the amount withheld to the Inland Revenue Authority of Singapore (hereinafter 'IRAS').

337. For example, a sports event is held in Singapore, in which a foreign athlete participates for a fee. The athlete brings an entourage, including a coach and a physiotherapist. Their fees, travel costs, accommodation and food are fully paid for by the organiser of the sports event. The athlete is classified as a non-resident public entertainer,[377] and his coach and physiotherapist are classified as non-resident professionals.[378]

338. The non-resident professional's gross income attributable to services rendered in Singapore is subject to withholding tax at a rate of 15%, or the non-resident rate of 24% if the non-resident professional has elected to be taxed on net income. Gross income refers to both cash and non-cash payments and includes accommodation, transport and meals that are provided or reimbursed by the payer, allowance and per diem payments. Net income refers to gross income less allowable expenses; the cost of airfare and the cost of accommodation for not more than sixty days in a calendar year are not taxable.

339. The non-resident professional may claim exemptions under tax treaties such as the Avoidance of Double Taxation Agreements made between Singapore and other nations. Qualifying conditions would have to be met. A person who wishes to claim an exemption must complete the relevant form and pass a hard copy to the payer. The payer claims the exemption on behalf of the non-resident professional.

340. The non-resident public entertainer is subject to a withholding tax at a rate of 15% on the taxable income from services performed in Singapore. This rate is reduced to 10% if the income is due and payable to the non-resident public entertainer during the period from 22 February 2010 to 31 March 2020. Taxable income refers to both cash and non-cash payments and includes match fees, prize money, tournament winnings, win bonuses, allowances, benefits-in-kind and non-cash gifts or prizes that exceed SGD 100. The cost of airfare and the cost of accommodation for not more than sixty days in a calendar year are not taxable.

341. The non-resident public entertainer may claim a full exemption from tax in Singapore if the Government of his home country substantially funded (i.e., more than 50%) of the visit. The payer does not need to withhold tax. The non-resident public entertainer must provide the supporting information to IRAS over email.

---

377. Inland Revenue Authority of Singapore, *Non-resident Public Entertainer*, https://www.iras.gov.sg/taxes/withholding-tax/payments-to-non-resident-public-entertainer-(artiste-musician-sportsman-etc-)/non-resident-public-entertainer (accessed 23 Nov. 2023).
378. Inland Revenue Authority of Singapore, *Non-resident Professionals*, https://www.iras.gov.sg/taxes/withholding-tax/payments-to-non-resident-professional-(consultant-trainer-coach-etc-)/non-resident-professional (accessed 23 Nov. 2023).

Part III. Doping and Sports

Chapter 1. Introduction

342. In simple terms, doping is the use of substances with the aim of artificially increasing performance for a sports event. It gives the taker an advantage over a fellow competitor who has not taken substances and therefore amounts to cheating. Furthermore, doping can affect the image and popularity of the sports, since it leads to an uneven playing field.

343. Singapore has few known cases of doping, but instances have occurred. Seven bodybuilders were banned in August 2012 for two years after testing positive for prohibited drugs in a local competition.[379] A silat athlete was banned with effect from 4 June 2013 for a two-year period after being unable to provide evidence on how banned substances had entered her system and failing to prove that the banned substances were present in traditional medicine that she took for back pain.[380] In April 2018, a sprinter became Singapore's first para-athlete to be banned for doping, following an out-of-competition test.[381] In May 2019, a local marathon winner was suspended from competition for three years and nine months by the International Association of Athletics Federation's Athletics Integrity Unit for consuming a quarter of one tablet of a banned substance on the morning of the event; the athlete's explanation that she had no intention to cheat because the substance was consumed to stay awake was not considered sufficient or credible.[382]

344. Unsurprisingly, the international community condemns doping and has implemented rules and policies to harmonise efforts to tackle the problem of drugs

379. SportSG (7 Aug. 2012), *Two-Year Ban for Seven Bodybuilding Athletes Who Tested Positive for Prohibited Substances*, https://www.sportsingapore.gov.sg/Newsroom/Media-Releases/2012/8/Two-Year-Ban-For-Seven-Bodybuilding-Athletes-Who-Tested-Positive-For-Prohibited-Substances (accessed 8 Jan. 2019).
380. SportSG (23 Jul. 2013), *Two-Year Ban for Silat Exponent Saiedah Said Upheld*, https://www.sportsingapore.gov.sg/newsroom/media-releases/2013/7/two-year-ban-for-silat-exponent-saiedah-said-upheld (accessed 8 Jan. 2019).
381. Wong, Jonathan (25 Apr. 2018), *Commonwealth Games: Singapore para athlete Khairi Ishak banned after failing dope test*, https://www.straitstimes.com/sport/commonwealth-games-singapore-para-athlete-khairi-ishak-banned-after-failing-dope-test, The Straits Times (accessed 8 Jan. 2019).
382. Athletics Integrity Unit (15 May 2019), *Decision of the Athletics Integrity Unit in the case of Ms Bao Ying Lim*, https://www.athleticsintegrity.org/downloads/pdfs/disciplinary-process/en/AIU-18-295-Baoying-LIM-AIU-decision.pdf, at para. 13.2 (accessed 29 Mar. 2021).

in sports. Locally, Singapore has also taken steps that demonstrate its commitment to ensuring that sports in Singapore is free from doping.

§1. International Level

345. The World Anti-Doping Agency (hereinafter 'WADA') was established in November 1999 as a foundation under the initiative of the IOC to promote and coordinate the international fight against doping.

346. In March 2003, more than a thousand delegates and observers descended into Copenhagen, Denmark, to attend the World Conference on Doping in Sport. On 5 March 2003, fifty-one nations signed the Copenhagen Declaration on Anti-Doping in Sport. Through the Declaration, the signatories agreed to recognise the role of, and support, WADA and to support the WAD Code. Furthermore, each signatory agreed that it 'recognises the role of the WAD Code as the foundation in the worldwide fight against doping in sport'[383] and 'seeks to progressively adapt, where appropriate, their anti-doping policies and practices in sport to be in conformity with the provisions of the WAD Code'.[384] Each signatory further agreed to sustained international cooperation to combat doping in sports. To date, Singapore is among the 193 countries that have signed the Declaration.

347. The WAD Code first entered into force on 1 January 2004. It was subsequently amended four times. A revised 2021 WAD Code came into effect on 1 January 2021.

348. Pursuant to the WAD Code, governments cooperated to create the International Convention Against Doping in Sport under the auspices of the United Nations Educational, Scientific and Cultural Organisation (commonly known as 'UNESCO'). The Convention was unanimously adopted at the UNESCO General Conference on 19 October 2005 and came into force on 1 February 2007. Singapore acceded to the Convention on 5 November 2007.

§2. Regional Level

349. At a regional level, WADA seeks to develop a clean sports culture through its Regional Anti-Doping Organization (hereinafter 'RADO') programme. Singapore is a participating member of the Southeast Asia RADO (hereinafter 'SEARADO'), which also includes Bruni Darussalam, Cambodia, Indonesia, Laos,

383. Copenhagen Declaration on Anti-Doping in Sport, Art. 4.1.
384. *Ibid.*, Art. 4.2.

Malaysia, Myanmar, the Philippines, Thailand, Timor-Lest and Vietnam. The Southeast RADO was established on 30 November 2006.[385] Its headquarters are in Singapore.[386]

350. The mission of the SEARADO is to promote and coordinate the fight against doping of all forms in sports in Southeast Asia.[387] The SEARADO collaborates and assists member countries with conducting Doping Control Officer training programmes and accreditation courses, in carrying out Out-of-Competition Testing.[388]

§3. National Level

351. ADS was established in 2010 by the MCCY as Singapore's national anti-doping organisation. ADS is a division within SportSG. ADS accepted the WAD Code on 24 February 2010.

352. As the country's national anti-doping organisation, ADS is responsible for planning, coordinating and implementing an effective doping control programme. To honour Singapore's commitment to the WAD Code, the Anti-Doping Policy of Singapore (hereinafter the 'AD Policy') and ADS Anti-Doping Rules (hereinafter the 'AD Rules') were developed. The articles in the AD Rules are based on the provisions in the WAD Code. All NSAs must accept and abide by the AD Rules and incorporate the AD Rules either directly or by reference into their governing documents, constitution and/or rules as a condition precedent of financial and/or other assistance from the Government of Singapore and/or the SNOC.[389]

353. All NSAs, athletes and athlete support personnel participating in events and competitions must observe and comply with the AD Policy and the AD Rules. This compliance is monitored by ADS. ADS is also responsible for coordinating Singapore's testing programme. Sanctions for violating anti-doping rules can range from disqualification of results to a lifetime ban.

354. In addition, athletes who traffic, import, export, possess or consume controlled drugs and substances in Singapore may be charged with criminal offences under the Misuse of Drugs Act (hereinafter 'MDAct'). Depending on the type and gravity of the offence, a conviction can result in punishment ranging from fines, caning, imprisonment and/or capital punishment. The MDAct also has extraterritorial reach – under section 8A, it is an offence for a Singapore citizen or a permanent resident of Singapore to consume a controlled drug even when the act takes place outside Singapore.

---

385. https://www.searado.com/about-searado/ (accessed 4 Apr. 2019).
386. *Ibid.*
387. *Ibid.*
388. https://www.searado.com/anti-doping-services/ (accessed 4 Apr. 2019).
389. AD Rules (version 1.3), Art. 18.2 and 18.3.

355. The results of a study titled *Attitudes, Beliefs, and Behaviors of Elite Singapore Athletes Towards Doping*[390] was published on 27 December 2018 on the SEARADO website.[391] The study 'investigated the current attitudes, beliefs, and behaviors of elite Singapore athletes towards doping'.[392] A total of 245 of Singapore's carded athletes had responded to a standardised survey from a WADA Social Science Research Package. The study found that a majority of athletes responded that they would not consider using performance-enhancing substances, even when the consequences of using them were not present.[393] A total of 92.1% of athletes further responded that they were confident of refusing any offer to use performance-enhancing substances,[394] and 98.7% of athletes self-reported as having never used any performance-enhancing substances in their sporting career.[395]

---

390. Dr Swarup Mukherjee, *Attitudes, Beliefs, and Behaviors of Elite Singapore Athletes Towards Doping* (accessible at https://www.searado.com/wp-content/uploads/2018/12/Attitudes-behaviours-of-elite-Singapore-athletes-towards-doping.pdf) (accessed 4 Apr. 2019).
391. https://www.searado.com/research/ (accessed 4 Apr. 2019).
392. *Attitudes, Beliefs, and Behaviors of Elite Singapore Athletes Towards Doping*, Summary.
393. *Attitudes, Beliefs, and Behaviors of Elite Singapore Athletes Towards Doping*, p. 11.
394. *Ibid.*
395. *Ibid.*, p. 12.

Chapter 2. The Anti-doping Policy of Singapore and the ADS Anti-doping Rules

356. The Introduction to the AD Rules sets out the persons to whom the AD Rules apply. They include:

- all athletes and athlete support personnel (such as a coach, trainer, manager or team staff) who are members of an NSA;
- all athletes and athlete support personnel who participate in events and competitions organised, convened, authorised or recognised by an NSA;
- any other athlete or athlete support personnel who is subject to the jurisdiction of an NSA by virtue of an accreditation, a licence or other contractual arrangement;
- all athletes and athlete support personnel who participate in a national event;
- recreational athletes; and
- all other athletes who are nationals or residents of Singapore, and all athletes who are present in Singapore, whether to compete, train or otherwise.

357. ADS has In-Competition and Out-of-Competing Testing authority over all of the athletes listed above.[396]

358. Anti-doping rule violations include but are not limited to situations where (a) there is presence of a prohibited substance or its metabolites or markers in an athlete's sample, and a Therapeutic Use Exemption does not apply to that substance and that athlete; (b) the athlete evades, refuses or fails to submit to a sample collection; (c) the athlete misses three tests within a twelve-month period; (d) the athlete tampers or attempts to tamper with the doping control process; or (e) the athlete possesses a prohibited substance.[397] The substances that are banned under the AD Rules[398] are identical to those set out in the Prohibited List that is published and revised by WADA.[399]

359. An anti-doping rule violation is committed on the basis of strict liability, i.e., without regard to the athlete's fault.[400] The burden of proof falls on ADS.[401] The standard of proof is greater than a balance of probability but is less than proof beyond a reasonable doubt;[402] it is comparable to the standard applied in cases involving professional misconduct.[403]

396. AD Rules (version 1.3), Art. 5.2.1.
397. *Ibid.*, Art. 2.
398. *Ibid.*, Art. 4.1.
399. The Prohibited List may be accessed at https://www.wada-ama.org/en/content/what-is-prohibited.
400. AD Rules (version 1.3), comment to Art. 2.1.1.
401. AD Rules (version 1.3), Art. 3.1.
402. *Ibid.*
403. AD Rules (version 1.3), comment to Art. 3.1.

360. In the event that a potential anti-doping rule violation occurs, ADS must carry out the review and notification in accordance with WADA'S International Standard for Results Management.[404]

361. The person will be given a chance to dispute the assertion of an anti-doping rule violation before a fair and impartial Hearing Panel. The Hearing Panel must comprise three persons and must include one qualified lawyer and one qualified medical practitioner.[405] After the hearing, a written decision will be issued[406] and provided to the person.[407] The decision can be appealed.[408]

362. Consequences of an anti-doping rule violation can include (a) invalidation of results and forfeiture of all medals, points and prizes; (b) suspension; or (c) a lifetime ban.[409] If more than two members of a team in a team sport have committed an anti-doping rule violation during an event period, then the team itself can also be sanctioned with consequences such as loss of points, or disqualification from the competition or event.[410]

363. Once the decision is final, the ADS must publicly report the sports, the anti-doping rule violated, the name of the person committing the violation, the prohibited substance or prohibited method involved (if any) and the consequences imposed.[411] Publication shall be accomplished at a minimum by publishing the required information on ADS' website for at least one month.[412]

364. No anti-doping rule violation proceeding may be commenced against a person if he or she has not been notified of the violation, or no notification has been reasonably attempted, within ten years from the date that the violation is asserted to have occurred.[413]

365. All NSAs must accept and abide by the AD Rules and incorporate the AD Rules either directly or by reference into their governing documents, constitution and/or rules as a condition precedent of financial and/or other assistance from the Government of Singapore and/or the SNOC.[414] This is achieved by signing the ADS' Collective Policy,[415] under which the NSA agrees to at all times:

404. AD Rules (version 1.3), Art. 7.2.
405. *Ibid.*, Art. 8.1.1 and 8.1.2.2.
406. *Ibid.*, Art. 8.2.1.
407. *Ibid.*, Art. 8.2.2.
408. *Ibid.*, Art. 13.
409. *Ibid.*, Art. 10.
410. *Ibid.*, Art. 11.2.
411. *Ibid.*, Art. 14.3.2.
412. *Ibid.*, Art. 14.3.5.
413. *Ibid.*, Art. 16.
414. *Ibid.*, Art. 18.2 and Art. 18.3.
415. An example of the Collective Policy may be viewed at https://www.singtennis.org.sg/page.aspx?url=general-policies/anti-doping-policy (accessed 18 Aug. 2021).

(a) recognise and accept the ADS as the National Anti-Doping Organisation designated by the Singapore Government as having the responsibility for all doping matters relating to sports in Singapore;
(b) accept the AD Policy and the AD Rules, both of which are established in accordance with the WAD Code, as the basis for the fight against doping in sports;
(c) adopt the AD Policy and the AD Rules either directly or by reference into the NSA's governing documents, constitution and/or rules and regulations, and which shall have binding force and effect on the NSA's members and participants; and
(d) agree to observe, abide by and implement the provisions of the AD Policy and the AD Rules in respect of the NSA's affairs and activities.

366. Failure by an NSA to abide by the spirit and terms of the ADS' Anti-Doping Programme, AD Rules and AD Policy could result in the withholding of financial support and further sanctions by the MCCY and SNOC regarding the eligibility of athletes and athlete support personnel participating in events and competitions.

Chapter 3. The Misuse of Drugs Act

367. Aside from facing sanctions for violating anti-doping rules, athletes may also face criminal sanctions if they breach the MDAct.

§1. OFFENCES

368. Singapore is well known for having extremely strict and tough drug laws. The mere possession of a very small amount of a controlled drug can result in a criminal conviction and a sentence of imprisonment. If a person is caught in possession of a relatively low amount of a controlled drug, he can be presumed to have had that drug in possession for the purpose of trafficking unless he can prove that his possession of that drug was not for trafficking.[416]

369. Section 5 of the MDAct makes it an offence to traffic, to offer to traffic, or to do or offer to do any act preparatory to or for the purpose of trafficking, in a controlled drug. In turn, the term 'traffic' is given a very wide definition in section 2 of the MDAct: to 'traffic' means 'to sell, give, administer, transport, send, deliver or distribute', or to offer to do any of these acts. The concept of trafficking involves transfer of possession and imports the existence of at least two parties: a supplier and a person to whom the goods are to be supplied.[417]

370. Section 6 of the MDAct makes it an offence to manufacture a controlled drug. Section 7 of the MDAct makes it an offence to import into or export from Singapore a controlled drug.

371. Section 8 of the MDAct makes it an offence for a person to have a controlled drug in his possession, or to consume a controlled or a specified drug. Section 9 criminalises the possession of utensils intended for the consumption of a controlled drug.

372. Section 11 of the MDAct makes it an offence for a person to allow premises of which he is the owner, tenant, occupier, or person-in-charge to be used for the consumption, trafficking or manufacturing of a controlled drug.

373. The First Schedule of the MDAct lists the drugs that are deemed 'controlled drugs'. These include amphetamine, cannabis, cocaine, diamorphine (commonly known as heroin), ecstasy, gamma-hydroxybutyric acid (commonly known as the date rape drug, or GHB), ketamine, morphine and oxycodone (just to name a few). 'Specified drugs' are listed in the Fourth Schedule of the MDAct and comprise a subset of the controlled drugs.

---

416. Misuse of Drugs Act, s. 17.
417. *Ong Ah Chuan v. Public Prosecutor* [1979-1980] SLR(R) 710, at para. 10.

§2. CONSEQUENCES OF A CONVICTION

374. The consequences of a conviction are set out in the Second Schedule of the MDAct and can include a fine, caning, imprisonment and/or capital punishment.

375. Pursuant to section 34 of the MDAct, a person reasonably suspected of being a drug addict can be sent to a Drug Rehabilitation Centre instead of being prosecuted in Court. Based on statements made in Parliament on 15 January 2019 during the Second Reading of the Misuse of Drugs (Amendment) Bill,[418] this provision is targeted at drug abusers who confess to consumption offences and do not face other criminal charges. Previously, repeat offenders would be sentenced to imprisonment and caning. With the amendments, repeat offenders will instead remain in a Drug Rehabilitation Centre for increasingly longer periods of time, depending on the number of times that they have previously offended, up to a maximum of four years. After release, the person would be placed on one of the three community-based programmes (i.e., sent to a halfway house, given day release from a community supervision centre or allowed home supervision with electronic tagging). Following the completion of the community-based programme, the person will be placed under supervision of up to five years. For those who deny consuming drugs or who commit other criminal offences, first-time offenders face a mandatory imprisonment term of one year, with longer terms of imprisonment being imposed for repeat offenders.[419]

376. In the event that a foreigner who is in Singapore on a work or visit pass is convicted under the MDAct and is sentenced to a term of imprisonment, it is highly likely that he will be deported from Singapore after he has served his sentence as he may be deemed a 'prohibited immigrant' (as defined under section 8 of the Immigration Act). If the person convicted is a permanent resident of Singapore, the Immigration Controller has the discretion to cancel the person's entry permit on the basis that the person is now an undesirable immigrant; if this takes place, then the person must leave Singapore or he is liable to be removed by the authorities.

418. *Singapore Parliamentary Report,* vol. 94, sitting no. 88, https://sprs.parl.gov.sg/search/#/sprs3topic?reportid=bill-347 (accessed 30 Jan. 2019).
419. MDAct, s. 33.

Part IV. Sports and Commerce

Chapter 1. Introduction

377. In the past two decades, Singapore has played host to several high-profile events, including the FIA Formula One Singapore Grand Prix, the World Rugby Singapore Sevens and the Women's Tennis Association Finals. It also hosted the Summer Youth Olympic Games in 2010 and matches for the 2018 International Champions Cup.

378. Hosting of such events has contributed to Singapore's economy. Since the inaugural FIA Formula One race in 2008, Singapore has hosted more than 550,000 international visitors, contributing about SGD 1.5 billion in incremental tourism receipts.[420] The race has also generated business opportunities for local companies, with more than 90% of race-related works subcontracted to Singapore-based companies.[421] When Singapore submitted its bid to host the Women's Tennis Association Finals, it was estimated that the event would generate tourism receipts of about SGD 15 million per year.[422] For the World Rugby Singapore Sevens, it was reported that the 2017 event generated a total economic impact of SGD 23.5 million.[423]

379. In March 2001, the Minister for Community Development and Sports announced in Parliament the intention to redevelop Singapore's National Stadium into an integrated sports hub. The vision was to 'provide Singaporeans with a world-class venue to watch top level sports, as well as provide excellent facilities for sports participation'.[424] The Singapore Sports Hub began operations in June 2014, with its

420. Mr Gan Kim Yong (2 Aug. 2023), *Singapore Parliamentary Report,* vol. 95, sitting no. 109, https://sprs.parl.gov.sg/search/#/sprs3topic?reportid=written-answer-na-14068 (accessed 23 Nov. 2023).
421. Mr S Iswaran (3 Oct. 2017), *Singapore Parliamentary Report,* vol. 94, sitting no. 52, https://sprs.parl.gov.sg/search/#/sprs3topic?reportid=written-answer-3947 (accessed 16 Jan. 2019).
422. Mr S Iswaran (13 May 2013), *Singapore Parliamentary Report,* vol. 90, sitting no. 18, https://sprs.parl.gov.sg/search/#/sprs3topic?reportid=written-answer-na-1330 (accessed 16 Jan. 2019).
423. Lin Fhoong, Low (4 Mar. 2018), *Home Is Where the Ruck Is, as S'pore Rugby 7s Aims to Stay at Sports Hub*, https://www.todayonline.com/singapore/home-where-ruck-spore-rugby-7s-aims-stay-sports-hub (accessed 16 Jan. 2019).
424. Mr Abdullah Tarmugi (14 Mar. 2001), *Singapore Parliamentary Report,* vol. 73, sitting no. 9 col. 1084, https://sprs.parl.gov.sg/search/#/topic?reportid=006_20010314_S0003_T0003 (accessed 16 Jan. 2019).

official opening taking place on 25 July 2015. It cost SGD 1.3 billion to construct[425] and contains several facilities, such as an aquatic centre, water sports centre, retail mall, skate park, sports library, museum and restaurants.

380. Given the recent increase in sports business and awareness in Singapore, there is currently no specific law that protects sports-related commercial rights. For example, there is no statute that addresses the issues that may arise in sports-related sponsorship and merchandising agreements, and the case law surrounding these areas is somewhat thin. Nevertheless, there is robust statutory and common law protection in place that enforces intellectual property rights generally.

381. On the criminal front, Singapore continues to keep up with technological advancements, such as by legislating the Gambling Control Act 2022 (GCA) (which consolidated a number of gambling-related Acts, including the Remote Gambling Act 2014) and Organised Crime Act 2015 (OCA) to target those who make use of online and/or syndicated means to carry out their illicit activities.

425. Bouygues Construction (25 Aug. 2010), *Bouygues Construction Signs a PPP Deal Worth 770 Million Euros for the Singapore Sports Hub*, https://www.bouygues-construction.com/en/press/release/bouygues-construction-signs-ppp-deal-worth-770-million-euros-singapore-sports-hub (accessed 16 Jan. 2019).

Chapter 2. Media and Television Rights

382. Sports events are broadcast on television, or via the Internet, or through an amalgamation of the two. In terms of television, MediaCorp Singapore (hereinafter 'MediaCorp') currently holds a monopoly on free-to-air channels, whereas pay television is operated by Singtel and StarHub Ltd (hereinafter 'StarHub'). Over the Internet, sports events can be watched legally or illegally. The former includes streaming on Internet television websites and mobile phone applications operated by MediaCorp, Singtel and StarHub. The latter includes unauthorised live streaming by websites which do not have a broadcasting licence issued by the Info-communications Media Development Authority of Singapore (hereinafter 'IMDA'). Television streaming boxes, which grant access to the Internet and various applications via a television screen, allow viewers to watch sports events on their television screens instead of a computer/laptop/mobile screen.

383. Singapore has taken steps to block access to illegal television streaming boxes. In November 2018, pursuant to a motion filed in October 2018 by a number of parties,[426] the Singapore High Court ordered Internet service providers to block access to television streaming boxes that allow users to stream and download content, including live sports channels.[427] These boxes are sold pre-loaded with applications to stream audiovisual content from illegal streaming servers, allowing consumers to access unauthorised premium television channels, live sports channels and movies for the one-off price of the television box and typically a yearly subscription to access the content.

384. In January 2019, it was jointly announced by the Ministry of Law and the Intellectual Property Office of Singapore (hereinafter 'IPOS')[428] that new laws would be tabled in Parliament in 2019 *inter alia* to ban the sale of media streaming boxes with add-on services that help consumers to access pirated content. In particular, the proposed new law would impose civil and criminal liability on people who wilfully make, import for sale, commercially distribute or sell a product, where the product can be used to access audiovisual content from an unauthorised source and additionally must be (a) designed or made primarily to access such content, or (b) advertised as providing access to such content, or (c) sold as providing access to such content, where the retailer sells a generic device with the understanding that add-on services such as the provision of website links or instructions or installation of subscription services to pirated content will be subsequently provided.

385. Also in January 2019, the English Football Premier League opened its first international office in Singapore. It 'has primarily been established to fight piracy

426. Namely, SingNet, Fox Networks Group Singapore, NGC Network Asia, Fox International Channels (US) and the Football Association Premier League.
427. Lay, Belmont (24 Nov. 2018), *Internet service providers in S'pore to block access to TV box apps s*, Mothership, https://mothership.sg/2018/11/tv-box-app-blocked-singapore/ (accessed 16 Jan. 2019).
428. Ministry of Law and IPOS (17 Jan. 2019), *Singapore Copyright Review Report*, https://www.mlaw.gov.sg/files/news/public-consultations/2021/copyrightbill/Annex_A-Copyright_Report 2019.pdf, at p. 67.

of Premier League content and support broadcast partners'.[429] One method used in the United Kingdom is for the Premier League to provide an Internet service provider with the IP addresses used to host illegal streams of the Premier League's matches, allowing the provider to block the streaming servers in real time. If the stream jumps to another IP address to evade the block, the Premier League is able to monitor such movements and dynamically block the new IP addresses as they migrate during the match.

386. Obtaining legal viewing access to sports events, however, can be expensive, and on occasion, to the point that persons in Singapore are unable to watch certain events live. For example, the 2006 Commonwealth Games were originally not due to be aired, with MediaCorp citing high costs as one of the reasons. The Media Development Authority and the SSC then provided funding, enabling live broadcasts to commence from the fourth day of competition.[430]

387. Similarly, the 2016 Indian Premier League, which is a seven-week cricket event, was not scheduled to be shown live in Singapore. Singtel blamed the rights holder for prohibitive costs,[431] while StarHub relented amid criticism on social media and secured the rights to televise the matches live starting on 18 April 2016, days after the event began on 9 April 2016.[432]

388. In another example, on 22 July 2016, MediaCorp announced that it would offer free limited coverage of the 2016 Summer Olympics held in Rio de Janeiro on digital, television, radio and print platforms. The announcement stated that coverage would include 'sport highlights, delayed telecast of up to twelve hours of games coverage daily and up-to-the-minute news coverage of Team Singapore's participation in the Games'.[433] The daily highlights could also be watched on a 'catch-up' basis on MediaCorp's online service platform Toggle. The opening and closing ceremonies would also be telecast live.

389. This led to a furore, as no paid television service provider was on the cards to provide live coverage of the Games. It was reported that the broadcast rights

429. Premier League (14 Jan. 2019), *Premier League Opens Asia-Pacific Office in Singapore*, https://www.premierleague.com/news/974802 (accessed 22 Jan. 2019).
430. The Straits Times (25 Jul. 2016), *How the Costs of Sports Broadcast Rights Have Shot Up in Singapore*, https://www.straitstimes.com/sport/how-the-costs-of-sports-broadcast-rights-have-shot-up-in-singapore (accessed 16 Jan. 2019).
431. Nair, Sanjay (10 Apr. 2016), *Cricket Fans in Singapore Unhappy with Lack of Indian Premier League Coverage on Cable TV*, The Straits Times, https://www.straitstimes.com/sport/cricket-fans-in-singapore-unhappy-with-lack-of-indian-premier-league-coverage-on-cable-tv (accessed 16 Jan. 2019).
432. The Straits Times (25 Jul. 2016), *How the Costs of Sports Broadcast Rights Have Shot Up in Singapore*, https://www.straitstimes.com/sport/how-the-costs-of-sports-broadcast-rights-have-shot-up-in-singapore (accessed 16 Jan. 2019).
433. MediaCorp (22 Jul. 2016), *MediaCorp Announces Dedicated Programmes and Digital Initiatives to Bring Rio 2016 Olympic Games to Singapore Audiences*, https://www.mediacorp.sg/corporate/news-release/media-releases/mediacorp-announces-dedicated-programmes-and-digital-initiatives-6475118 (accessed 16 Jan. 2019).

holder Dentsu Inc.'s asking price was in the region of USD 6 million, more than double the sum that MediaCorp had paid for broadcasting the 2012 Olympic Games held in London (which was reportedly about USD 2.5 million).[434]

390. Subsequently, on 5 August 2016, MediaCorp announced that it had made 'an eleventh-hour deal … for Olympic Games live broadcast rights in Singapore'.[435] This allowed Singapore citizens and residents to (legally) watch Joseph Schooling swim to win the nation's first Olympics gold medal.

§1. Regulation

391. Regulation of the television industry and Internet services is carried out by the IMDA, which is a statutory board. The IMDA was formed on 1 October 2016 through the merger of the Infocomm Development Authority and the Media Development Authority. The functions of the IMDA are set out in section 5 of the Info-communications Media Development Authority Act 2016 (hereinafter 'IMDAA') and include but are not limited to the following:

- to promote the efficiency, competitiveness (including internationally) and development of the information, communications and media industry in Singapore;
- to promote and maintain fair and efficient market conduct and effective competition between persons engaged in commercial activities in connection with media services or telecommunication systems and services in Singapore or, in the absence of a competitive market, to prevent the misuse of monopoly or market power;
- to regulate the provision and use of telecommunication systems and media services in Singapore;
- to promote the use of the Internet and electronic commerce in Singapore and to establish regulatory frameworks for that purpose;
- to promote, where suitable, self-regulation in the information, communications and media industry in Singapore.

392. The persons who are regulated under the IMDAA are newspaper companies and holders of a broadcasting licence.[436] The latter includes providers of free-to-air television services, paid television services, free-to-air radio services, paid radio services and computer online services provided by Internet content providers and Internet service providers.[437]

434. The Straits Times (25 Jul. 2016), *How the Costs of Sports Broadcast Rights Have Shot Up in Singapore*, https://www.straitstimes.com/sport/how-the-costs-of-sports-broadcast-rights-have-shot-up-in-singapore (accessed 16 Jan. 2019).

435. MediaCorp (5 Aug. 2016), *MediaCorp Adds Live Coverage to Schedule of Comprehensive Rio 2016 Content*, https://www.mediacorp.sg/corporate/news-release/media-releases/mediacorp-adds-live-coverage-to-schedule-of-comprehensive-rio-6510704 (accessed 16 Jan. 2019).

436. IMDAA, s. 2.

437. *See* (i) Media Development Authority of Singapore (Regulated Persons) Notification 2003, (ii) Broadcasting Act (Cap 28), Second Schedule and (iii) Section 9, Broadcasting Act (Cap 28) read with Broadcasting (Class Licence) Notification.

§2. Code of Practice for Market Conduct

393. Pursuant to section 61(7) of the IMDAA, all regulated persons must comply with any code of practice issued by the IMDA. Before the merger that formed the IMDA, the Media Development Authority had exercised its power under section 17(2) of the Media Development Authority of Singapore Act (Cap 172) and issued a Code of Practice for Market Conduct in the Provision of Media Services (hereinafter 'Conduct Code') on 1 April 2003. Under section 90(2) of the IMDAA, the Conduct Code remains in force and is deemed to have been issued by the IMDA.

394. The goals of the Conduct Code are listed in Clause 1.1 of the Code, as follows:

(a) enable and maintain fair market conduct and effective competition in Singapore's media industry;
(b) ensure the availability of a comprehensive range of quality media services in Singapore;
(c) encourage industry self-regulation in Singapore's media industry;
(d) foster further investment in and the development of Singapore's media industry; and
(e) safeguard the public interest.

§3. Anti-siphoning Scheme

395. The Conduct Code introduced an anti-siphoning scheme that prevents the siphoning of certain sports events to pay television at the expense of viewers who use only free-to-air television. Under the anti-siphoning scheme, subscription television licensees are restricted from acquiring certain exclusive broadcast rights for programmes. The programmes in question are listed in an anti-siphoning list.

396. The anti-siphoning list classifies programmes into two categories: Category A and Category B. For Category A programmes, subscription television licensees cannot acquire exclusive live or delayed broadcast rights. For Category B programmes, subscription television licensees can acquire exclusive live, but not exclusive delayed, broadcast rights.[438]

397. Under Clause 2.6.1.3(d) of the Conduct Code, when determining which events fall under the anti-siphoning list, the IMDA will consider all relevant issues,

438. Media Development Authority of Singapore and SSC (20 Sep. 2012), *Proposed Revisions to the Anti-siphoning List and Definition of Delayed Broadcast – Public Consultation*, https://www.imda.gov.sg/-/media/imda/files/regulation-licensing-and-consultations/consultations/completed-consultations/consultation-papers/7/anti-siphoning-public-consultation.pdf?la=en (accessed 16 Jan. 2019).

including whether the programme involves major international sports events, international sports events in which a Singapore team or personality is participating, or significant local sports events.

398. Between February and August 2012, the Media Development Authority of Singapore convened a panel to review and propose revisions to the anti-siphoning list. A public consultation was launched on 20 September 2012. Both Singtel and StarHub provided input. As a result, the list was revised with effect from 11 January 2013.[439] Under the current list, Category A events comprise the Asian Games; the Commonwealth Games; the Singapore Grand Prix event in the FIA Formula One World Championship calendar; the opening, semi-final and final matches of the FIFA World Cup and any match that involves Team Singapore; the Southeast Asian Games; and the Summer Olympic Games. Category B events comprise the ASEAN Football Federation Suzuki Cup, matches during the Malaysia Cup that involve Singapore club teams, the Summer Paralympic Games and the Summer Youth Olympic Games.

399. As an example of the operation of the anti-siphoning scheme, on 25 April 2018, MediaCorp, Singtel and StarHub announced that they would be collaborating to broadcast the 2018 FIFA World Cup Russia event in Singapore, for a subscription fee that granted viewing access via television and online platforms.[440] In addition, MediaCorp was allowed to broadcast nine matches on a free-to-air channel, including the opening match, the semi-final matches and the final match.[441]

§4. Cross-Carriage Rule

400. Exclusive carriage agreements are not uncommon in the pay television market. They allow pay television providers to lock in premium content in exchange for the payment of a premium for exclusive rights to the content. This typically results in higher costs to the consumer. In a Parliamentary speech on 12 March 2010, the Acting Minister for Information, Communications and the Arts noted that following Singtel's entry into the pay television market in July 2007, competition between Singtel and StarHub had resulted in the number of exclusive carriage

439. Media Development Authority of Singapore and SSC (11 Jan. 2013), *Closing Note to Public Consultation on Revisions to the Anti-siphoning List and Definition of Delayed Broadcast*, https://www.imda.gov.sg/-/media/imda/files/regulation-licensing-and-consultations/frameworks-and-policies/conducive-media-environment/antisiphoning-closing-note-to-public-consultation-11-jan-2013.pdf (accessed 16 Jan. 2019).

440. MediaCorp (25 Apr. 2018), *Singtel, StarHub and MediaCorp to Broadcast 2018 FIFA World Cup Russia*™, https://www.mediacorp.sg/corporate/news-release/media-releases/singtel-starhub-and-mediacorp-to-broadcast-2018-fifa-world-cup-10173278 (accessed 16 Jan. 2019).

441. Channel NewsAsia (25 Apr. 2018), *MediaCorp, Singtel, StarHub to Broadcast 2018 World Cup*, https://www.channelnewsasia.com/news/singapore/world-cup-2018-football-toggle-MediaCorp-singtel-starhub-10171696 (accessed 16 Jan. 2019).

agreements doubling from 64 in December 2005 to 131 in March 2010.[442] The Acting Minister noted that an international benchmarking exercise conducted by his ministry with a group of sixteen popular channels showed that Singapore was the only country with exclusive arrangements for all sixteen channels.[443]

401. The problems brought about by exclusive carriage arrangements had come to a head a few months earlier, when on 1 October 2009 Singtel announced that it had won the bid for exclusive rights to broadcast English Premier League matches for three years commencing August 2010.[444] It had reportedly paid close to SGD 400 million for the rights, which was a 60% increase from the SGD 250 million paid by StarHub three years previously for the exclusive broadcast rights for the English Premier League's 2006 to 2009 season. Singtel's 2009 winning of the bid saw its subscription rate shoot up from about 155,000 to 400,000.[445]

402. Following letters and commentaries in the press, the Media Development Authority made a statement on 21 January 2010, 'encouraging SingTel, StarHub and MediaCorp to continue their negotiations with FIFA to telecast the World Cup in Singapore. We hope the negotiations will reach a sensible outcome that will benefit all football fans'.[446]

403. On 12 March 2010, the Media Development Authority revised the Conduct Code to incorporate a measure requiring pay television retailers to cross-carry each other's content which has been acquired exclusively.[447] For example, if retailer A acquires a new channel exclusively, it must make this channel exclusively for retailer B on retailer B's set-top box. The content continues to be branded in its

---

442. Mr Lui Tuck Yew (12 Mar. 2010), *Singapore Parliamentary Report,* vol. 86, sitting no. 25 col. 4281, available at https://sprs.parl.gov.sg/search/#/topic?reportid=007_20100312_S0004_T0002 (accessed 16 Jan. 2019).
443. Mr Lui Tuck Yew (12 Mar. 2010), *Singapore Parliamentary Report,* vol. 86, sitting no. 25 col. 4282, available at https://sprs.parl.gov.sg/search/#/topic?reportid=007_20100312_S0004_T0002 (accessed 16 Jan. 2019).
444. Singtel (1 Oct. 2009), *Singtel Wins Exclusive Rights to the Barclays Premier League*, https://www.singtel.com/about-us/media-centre/news-releases/singtel-wins-exclusive-rights-barclays-premier-league (accessed 16 Jan. 2019).
445. Wong, Adelene (12 Feb. 2015), *Premier League's S$10.6b TV Deal May Be Bad News for Fans*, Today, https://www.todayonline.com/sports/football/premier-leagues-s106b-tv-deal-may-be-bad-news-fans (accessed 16 Jan. 2019).
446. Media Development Authority of Singapore (21 Jan. 2010), *MDA's Response on World Cup Issue*, https://www.imda.gov.sg/resources/press-releases-factsheets-and-speeches/archived/mda/press-releases/2010/mdas-response-on-world-cup-issue (accessed 16 Jan. 2019).
447. Media Development Authority of Singapore (12 Mar. 2010), *Media Market Conduct Code Revised to Better Serve Consumers and Create More Opportunities for Industry Growth*, https://www.imda.gov.sg/resources/press-releases-factsheets-and-speeches/archived/mda/press-releases/2010/media-market-conduct-code-revised-to-better-serve-consumers-and-create-more-opportunities-for-industry-growth (accessed 16 Jan. 2019).

original form, featuring retailer A's branding and commercials.[448] Consumers can therefore watch an exclusive channel through their preferred pay television retailer without having to switch retailers.

404. This cross-carriage measure is mandatory. It is described in the Conduct Code as a 'public interest obligation' and is found in Clause 2.1.5 of the Conduct Code.

405. The cross-carriage measure was implemented from 1 August 2011 but applies to any pay TV retailer that has acquired any exclusive content on or after 12 March 2010.[449]

406. On 10 October 2012, Singtel announced that it had secured 'non-exclusive' rights to broadcast English Premier League matches for three years commencing August 2013.[450] However, the Media Development Authority examined the agreement and concluded that it contained price barrier and marketing restriction clauses that restricted the same content being acquired in Singapore by other pay television retailer.[451] As a result, on 24 April 2013, the Media Development Authority issued a direction to Singtel, requiring it to cross-carry the matches to StarHub's platform.[452] The first implementation of the cross-carriage measure occurred in 2012 when StarHub exclusively acquired the rights to the 2012 Union of European Football Associations Championship (commonly known as the 'Euro Championship') and the sixty-four matches were cross-carried to Singtel's platform.[453]

---

448. Media Development Authority of Singapore (18 May 2010), *MDA Clarifies Cross-Carriage of Exclusive Content*, https://www.imda.gov.sg/resources/press-releases-factsheets-and-speeches/archived/mda/press-releases/2010/mda-clarifies-crosscarriage-of-exclusive-content (accessed 16 Jan. 2019).
449. Media Development Authority of Singapore (1 Jul. 2011), *Cross-Carriage to Be Implemented from 1 August 2011*, https://www.imda.gov.sg/resources/press-releases-factsheets-and-speeches/archived/mda/press-releases/2011/crosscarriage-to-be-implemented-from-1-august-2011 (accessed 16 Jan. 2019).
450. Singtel (10 Oct. 2012), *Singtel Mio TV Secures Rights to Broadcast Barclays Premier League for Another Three Seasons*, https://www.singtel.com/about-us/media-centre/news-releases/singtel-mio-tv-secures-rights-broadcast-barclays-premier-league-another-three (accessed 16 Jan. 2019).
451. Media Development Authority of Singapore, *Summary of the Direction of the Media Development Authority of Singapore Made Pursuant to Section 26 (1) of the Media Development Authority of Singapore Act (Cap. 172)*, https://www.imda.gov.sg/-/media/imda/files/inner/about-us/newsroom/mda/information-circular-in-respect-of-the-crosscarriage-measure-summary-of-the-direction-to-singnet-to-crosscarry-the-barcla/finalsummary-of-direction.pdf?la=en (accessed 16 Jan. 2019).
452. Media Development Authority of Singapore (24 Apr. 2013), *MDA Directs SingNet to Cross-Carry Barclays Premier League 2013–2016 Seasons*, https://www.imda.gov.sg/resources/press-releases-factsheets-and-speeches/archived/mda/press-releases/2013/mda-directs-singnet-to-crosscarry-barclays-premier-league-2013--2016-seasons (accessed 16 Jan. 2019).
453. *Ibid.*

Chapter 3. Sponsorship

407. Sponsorship is an arrangement whereby one party (the sponsor) pays a certain sum of money (the sponsorship fee) to another party (the sponsored party), in exchange for certain rights of association with the sponsored party.

408. In sports, sponsorship is an attractive method of raising funds for athletes, clubs, associations and events. Sponsorship for a club allows it to engage good quality coaches, purchase or obtain the use of good training facilities and equipment and provide better insurance and medical benefits for its athletes. Similar benefits accrue to athletes, whether professional or amateur, who have sponsorship. For events, sponsorship provides funding for purposes such as renting the event venue, advertising the event, paying certain athletes for participation in the event and contributing to the prize money purse. Allied Market Research valued the global sports sponsorship market in 2022 at USD 73.8 billion, and projected it to reach USD 151.4 billion by 2023.[454]

409. The sponsor in turn enjoys the goodwill benefits brought about through its association with the sponsored party. Advertising and television and media coverage help to publicise the sponsor and bring its brand to a wider audience. Exclusive rights enjoyed by the sponsor may also directly contribute to its revenue, such as being the only brand allowed to sell beverages at a sponsored event.

410. Given that sponsorship can at times involve substantial investment into the sponsored party, sponsors may expect certain levels of protection of their investment. Ambush marketing, whereby a third party seeks to convey to the public the false or misleading impression that an association exists between the third party and a sponsored party, is naturally a concern for the sponsor.

411. In Singapore, there is no legislation that specifically governs sponsorship contracts. Rather, such contracts are governed by the principles of contract law. The sponsorship agreement need not be in writing; it can be in oral form.[455]

§1. Tobacco Sponsorship

412. The title of the anti-tobacco advertisement legislation in Singapore has evolved over the years. The provisions were first contained in the 1971 Smoking (Prohibition on Advertisements) Act (Cap 309), which was repealed in 1993 and replaced by the Smoking (Control of Advertisements and Sale of Tobacco) Act (Cap

454. Allied Market Research, *Sports Sponsorship Market Research, 2032*, https://www.alliedmarketresearch.com/sports-sponsorship-market-A121165 (accessed 23 Nov. 2023).

455. *See*, for example, *Excel Golf Pte Ltd v. Allied Domecq Spirits and Wine (Singapore) Ltd (No 2)* [2004] SGHC 162.

309). The title of the latter was changed to the Tobacco (Control of Advertisements and Sale) Act 1993 (hereinafter the 'Tobacco Act') in 2010 and remains known as such today.

413. In 1971, Singapore became the first country in Asia to ban advertising on tobacco.[456] In 1989, Parliament passed the Smoking (Prohibition on Advertisements) (Amendment) Bill. This Bill inserted a provision that allowed the Minister for Health to approve advertisements that mentioned the name of tobacco manufacturers or distributors as a sponsor of an event or in congratulatory messages.[457] It appears that this exemption was intended to be applied in practice in relation to tobacco sponsorship of arts and cultural events.[458]

414. In 2004, Singapore ratified the World Health Organisation Framework Convention on Tobacco Control (hereinafter the 'FCTC'). Article 13(2) of the FCTC mandates that '[e]ach Party shall, in accordance with its constitution or constitutional principles, undertake a comprehensive ban of all tobacco advertising, promotion and sponsorship. This shall include, subject to the legal environment and technical means available to that Party, a comprehensive ban on cross-border advertising, promotion and sponsorship originating from its territory'.

415. In order to comply with Article 13(2) of the FCTC, Parliament passed the Smoking (Control of Advertisements and Sale of Tobacco) (Amendment) Bill on 19 July 2010.[459] This removed the exemption that allowed the Minister for Health to approve advertisements that publicly acknowledged tobacco sponsorship.

416. Today, section 3(1)(d) of the Tobacco Act prohibits the publication of any advertisement in Singapore that mentions, illustrates or depicts the brand name or trade mark of, or pictorial device associated with, any tobacco product or imitation product. 'Advertisement' is widely defined in section 2(1) of the Tobacco Act as including any writing on any document or object and any oral notification.

417. As such, although tobacco sponsorship is not expressly prohibited in Singapore, the 2010 repeal of the sponsorship advertising exemption has in effect led to lack of tobacco sponsorship today. Section 3(2) of the Tobacco Act nevertheless allows the Minister for Health to approve advertisements that mention or refer to

---

456. Mr Khaw Boon Wan (19 Jul. 2010), *Singapore Parliamentary Report,* vol. 87, sitting no. 5 col. 669, available at https://sprs.parl.gov.sg/search/#/topic?reportid=015_20100719_S0004_T0006 (accessed 9 Jan. 2019).
457. *See* the Smoking (Prohibition on Advertisements) (Amendment) Act 1989, s. 3, available at https://sso.agc.gov.sg/Acts-Supp/36-1989/Published/19891208?DocDate=19891208 (accessed 9 Jan. 2019).
458. Mr Khaw Boon Wan (19 Jul. 2010), *Singapore Parliamentary Report,* vol. 87, sitting no. 5 col. 671, available at https://sprs.parl.gov.sg/search/#/topic?reportid=015_20100719_S0004_T0006 (accessed 9 Jan. 2019).
459. Mr Khaw Boon Wan (19 Jul. 2010), *Singapore Parliamentary Report,* vol. 87, sitting no. 5 col. 669, available at https://sprs.parl.gov.sg/search/#/topic?reportid=015_20100719_S0004_T0006 (accessed 9 Jan. 2019).

the name of tobacco manufacturers or distributors, where the advertisement's purpose is to promote or identify goods or services that are unconnected with tobacco products.

§2. Alcohol Sponsorship

418. There are no restrictions in Singapore against alcohol sponsorship. For example, the local beer brand Tiger Beer was announced as the official beer of the HSBC Singapore Rugby 7s tournament in 2017. The Thai brand Chang Beer was one of Singtel's broadcast sponsors for the 2016/17 English Premier League season. Carlsberg Beer and Glenfiddich Whisky were attributed as official supporters of the 2019 SMBC Singapore Open golf event.

419. However, Appendix K of the Singapore Code of Advertising Practice sets out certain guidelines regarding the advertising of alcoholic drinks. These guidelines include that (a) children should not be portrayed in advertisements for alcoholic drinks and (b) advertisements should not be directed at people under the age of 18 or in any way encourage them to start drinking. Similar guidelines are echoed at Clause 5.17 of the Television and Radio Advertising and Sponsorship Code. In practice, this means that alcohol advertisements are not shown during programmes intended for children and young persons. There appears to be no curtailment on the publicity of a sponsorship role played by alcohol companies.

§3. Naming Rights

420. One of the rights that may be granted to a sponsor is a naming right, i.e., the right to name a facility or event, typically for a defined period of time. This right caused public concern in November 2012, when it was announced that OCBC Bank had signed a Memorandum of Understanding with the consortium running the Singapore Sports Hub[460] that would allow OCBC to have naming rights to all facilities in the Sports Hub, including the existing Singapore Indoor Stadium.[461] It had been clarified by the then-Deputy Prime Minister in 2001 that banks were free to negotiate with owners of buildings for naming rights without needing to consult the Monetary Authority of Singapore.[462]

460. Namely, Sports Hub Pte Ltd. Since 9 Dec. 2022, ownership and management of the Singapore Sports Hub has been taken over by SportSG.
461. Meng Meng, Wang (29 Nov. 2012), *$80m for Sports Hub Naming Rights*, AsiaOne, http://www.asiaone.com/print/News/Latest%2BNews/Sports/Story/A1Story20121128-386215.html (accessed 9 Jan. 2019).
462. Mr Lee Hsien Loong (25 Sep. 2001), *Singapore Parliamentary Report,* vol. 73, sitting no. 18 col. 2072, available at https://sprs.parl.gov.sg/search/#/topic?reportid=010_20010925_S0006_T0020 (accessed 9 Jan. 2019).

421. On 6 February 2013, the MCCY clarified that under the contract with the SSC, the operator of the Sports Hub could sell the naming rights to individual facilities within the Sports Hub, except for the National Stadium. However, any sale of naming rights within the Sports Hub would still be subject to SSC's consent. The MCCY also stressed that the revenue from the sale of naming rights 'may be used to finance future enhancements to the facilities to have better events and shows as well as to fund community events and support the development of our athletes'.[463]

422. Further clarification was sought from the MCCY in August 2013. The MCCY explained that it had examined the naming rights proposal and 'decided that it was important to retain the over-riding principle of preserving the Sports Hub and the National Stadium as national icons free from commercial naming rights'. As such, naming rights could only be given to certain facilities within the Sports Hub.[464]

423. As such, on 11 November 2013, it was announced that the Sports Hub consortium had entered into a fifteen-year sponsorship deal with OCBC Bank, reportedly for a value of more than SGD 50 million.[465] Under the deal, OCBC Bank was granted naming rights for the Sports Hub's sports hall and aquatic centre and three lounges in the National Stadium and the Singapore Indoor Stadium.

424. The OCBC Bank Chairman candidly admitted that corporate social responsibility was not the sole motivating factor. He noted 'the immense commercial value of the naming rights and the prominent presence of OCBC in the iconic Sports Hub. When events of international standing are held at and televised from the Sports Hub, as they inevitably will be, the name of OCBC will be visible. This should keep our shareholders happy'.[466]

§4. Ambush Marketing

425. Ambush marketing is a practice where a third party seeks to convey to the public the false or misleading impression that an association exists between the third party and a sponsored party, when no such association exists. For example, during the Wimbledon tennis event in 2009, the potato crisp brand Pringles gave away

463. Mr Lawrence Wong (6 Feb. 2013), *Singapore Parliamentary Report* vol. 90 sitting no. 4, available at https://sprs.parl.gov.sg/search/#/topic?reportid=009_20130206_S0007_T0007 (accessed 9 Jan. 2019).
464. Mr Lawrence Wong (12 Aug. 2013), *Singapore Parliamentary Report,* vol. 90 sitting no. 21, available at https://sprs.parl.gov.sg/search/#/topic?reportid=029_20130812_S0015_T0020 (accessed 9 Jan. 2019).
465. Chen, May (11 Nov. 2013), *OCBC Secures $50 Million, 15-Year Naming Rights Deal as Main Sponsorship Partner of Singapore Sports Hub,* The Straits Times, https://www.straitstimes.com/sport/ocbc-secures-50-million-15-year-naming-rights-deal-as-main-sponsorship-partner-of-singapore (accessed 9 Jan. 2019).
466. OCBC Group (11 Nov. 2013), *OCBC Group Is the Largest Sponsorship Partner of Singapore Sports Hub,* https://www.ocbc.com/group/media/release/2013/ocbc-singapore-sports-hub-sponsorship.html (accessed 9 Jan. 2019).

more than 20,000 tubes of its products to spectators entering the Wimbledon grounds. The tubes bear a similar shape to tennis ball containers. The packaging contained the usual Pringles logo and brand name, together with the words, 'These are not tennis balls!'

426. In another example, during the 1996 Atlanta Olympic Games, at which Reebok was the official sponsor for the reported sum of USD 50 million,[467] Nike opened a 'Nike Centre' next to the athletes' village and distributed flags containing its swoosh logo to spectators. Conspicuously, it also provided gold-coloured shoes with its swoosh logo to sprinter Michael Johnson. He went on to win the Men's 200-metre and 400-metre events while wearing the shoes and was subsequently photographed for the 12 August 1996 cover of *TIME* magazine with the shoes hung around his neck.

427. In a local example, Joseph Schooling caused much excitement in Singapore when he clinched the nation's first gold in the Summer Olympic Games on 12 August 2016, in the Men's 100-metre butterfly swimming event where he clocked a swim time of 50.39 seconds. Several corporations immediately fired out congratulatory messages that also advertised their products. For example, Brand's (which flagship product is a chicken essence drink that is marketed as helping its consumers 'achieve greatness'[468]) published an advertisement stating, 'Years to prepare for greatness. 50.39 seconds to unlock it', together with an image of its chicken essence product.[469] McDonald's congratulated Schooling on 'winning his own golden nugget' and offered free Chicken McNuggets to the first fifty customers at its restaurants in Singapore.[470]

428. Other companies offered promotions, such as Canopy Garden Dining offering a 50.39% discount on meals,[471] and the private car-hire company Grab Singapore providing discounted rides to and from swimming complexes with the use of the promotion code 'SCHOOLING'.[472]

429. Ambush marketing can help to provide free advertising for an event and is an exercise in commercial free speech. However, given that sponsors can pay substantial sums of money that help to subsidise or cover the costs of holding sports

467. Klara, Robert (10 Aug. 2016), *How Nike Brilliantly Ruined Olympic Marketing Forever*, Adweek, https://www.adweek.com/brand-marketing/how-nike-brilliantly-ruined-olympic-marketing-forever-172899/ (accessed 10 Jan. 2019).
468. *See* the tagline 'Achieve greatness with BRAND'S® Essence of Chicken' at https://www.brandsworld.com.sg/en/products/essence-of-chicken-original.html (accessed 9 Jan. 2019).
469. A copy of the advertisement may be viewed at https://www.mrbrown.com/.a/6a00d83451b52369e201b8d210de49970c-popup (accessed 9 Jan. 2019).
470. A copy of the advertisement may be viewed at https://www.mrbrown.com/.a/6a00d83451b52369e201b7c8872eeb970b-popup (accessed 9 Jan. 2019).
471. A copy of the advertisement may be viewed at https://www.mrbrown.com/.a/6a00d83451b52369e201b7c8872ecf970b-popup (accessed 9 Jan. 2019).
472. A copy of the advertisement may be viewed at https://www.mrbrown.com/.a/6a00d83451b52369e201bb092a7f9b970d-popup (accessed 9 Jan. 2019).

events, sponsorship investment ought to be protected to ensure financial success and overall longevity of an event, which in turn promotes interest in the sports in question.

I. Intellectual Property Law

430. In Singapore, there is currently no law that specifically protects sponsorship rights. Where intellectual property is infringed, then such rights may be protected under the Trade Marks Act 1998 (TMA) or the Copyright Right 2021. In relation to the Olympics, according to Rule 7 of the Olympic Charter,[473] all rights (including intellectual property rights) relating to the Olympic Games and Olympic properties[474] belong exclusively to the IOC. The SNOC in turn is charged with oversight of the intellectual property rights associated with the Olympics at the national level. For example, the flurry of advertisements and promotions after Schooling's 2016 Olympic victory quickly triggered correspondence from the IOC to the SNOC, raising the issue of ambush marketing. The SNOC in turn wrote to companies to ask them to refrain from using Olympic-related images to market their own products.[475]

431. However, ambush marketing typically does not infringe intellectual property rights. Instead, it seeks to have a brand be associated in the mind of the consumer with an event, without actually referencing the event. For example, Adidas was the official sportswear sponsor for the 2012 London Olympic Games, reportedly paying around GBP 40 million for the deal.[476] Nike, which was not an official sponsor, released several advertisements around the period of the Games, featuring people playing sports in towns around the world named 'London'. There was no mention of the city of London where the Olympic Games were held nor of the Olympic Games.

II. Tort of Passing Off

432. Where intellectual property has not been infringed by an ambush marketer, the injured party may instead seek to rely on an action brought under the tort of passing off. The law of passing off prevents one party from misrepresenting goods

473. Version in force as from 15 Oct. 2023.

474. The Olympic properties include the Olympic symbol, flag, motto, anthem, identifications (such as 'Olympic Games' and 'Games of the Olympiad'), designations, emblems, flame, torches, and any other musical works, audiovisual works or other creative works or artefacts commissioned in connection with the Olympic Games by the IOC, the National Olympic Committees and/or the Organising Committees for the Olympic Games: Olympic Charter, Rule 7(4).

475. Osman, Shamir (18 Aug. 2016), *Singapore Flagged for Ambush Marketing*, The New Paper, http://www.asiaone.com/singapore/singapore-flagged-ambush-marketing (accessed 9 Jan. 2019).

476. The Guardian (19 Jul. 2012), *London 2012 Olympic Sponsors List: Who Are They and What Have They Paid?*, https://www.theguardian.com/sport/datablog/2012/jul/19/london-2012-olympic-sponsors-list (accessed 10 Jan. 2019).

or services as being the goods and services of another party. It also prevents one party from holding out his goods or services as having some association or connection with another party when this is not true. Three elements must be established in order to succeed in a passing-off action: goodwill, misrepresentation and damage.[477]

433. In *CDL Hotels International Ltd v. Pontiac Marina Pte Ltd* [1998] 1 SLR(R) 975, the Singapore Court of Appeal distinguished between goodwill and reputation holding that '[g]oodwill does not exist on its own and it attaches to a business. On the other hand, reputation may, and often does, exist without any supporting business'.[478] The court further noted that although goodwill is normally generated from trading,[479] pre-business activities can generate goodwill, such as when promoters of businesses embark on massive advertising campaigns before the commencement of trading to familiarise the public with the service or product.[480]

434. The parties in a passing-off action also need not be in mutual competition, although the plaintiff's case is strengthened where there is a common field of activity and the parties are in competition with each other.[481]

435. As regards misrepresentation, passing off requires that the defendant's action must have led or was likely to lead the public to believe that the goods or services offered by him are the goods or services of the plaintiff. Confusion is an essential element of the tort of passing off: although evidence of actual confusion is not required before a passing-off action can succeed, it is open to the court to infer a likelihood of confusion from the surrounding facts.[482]

436. One potential method, therefore, of avoiding being successfully litigated against in a passing-off action is for the defendant to include a disclaimer on all advertising material, stating that the defendant is not associated with or a sponsor of the sports event in question. The existence of such a disclaimer was one of the reasons that the passing-off claim against the defendant in the Canadian case of *National Hockey League et al. v. Pepsi-Cola Canada* (1992) 42 CPR (3d) 390 was dismissed.

437. Finally, the plaintiff must prove damage, i.e., that the misrepresentation has caused, or is likely to cause, damage to the plaintiff's goodwill.[483] There are two primary means by which goodwill can be damaged: namely, by blurring or by tarnishment.

---

477. *Novelty Pte Ltd v. Amanresorts Ltd* [2009] 3 SLR(R) 216, at para. 37.
478. At para. 46 of the judgment.
479. At para. 52 of the judgment.
480. At para. 58 of the judgment.
481. *CDL Hotels International Ltd v. Pontiac Marina Pte Ltd* [1998] 1 SLR(R) 975, at paras 63 and 65.
482. *Novelty Pte Ltd v. Amanresorts Ltd* [2009] 3 SLR(R) 216, at para. 77.
483. *Ibid.*, at para. 94.

438. Blurring occurs when the plaintiff's get-up, instead of being indicative of only the plaintiff's goods, services or business, also becomes indicative of the defendant's goods, services or business. The damage manifests itself in sales being diverted from the plaintiff to the defendant.[484]

439. Tarnishment occurs when the business, goods or services of the defendant are of a worse quality than those of the plaintiff or have some other undesirable characteristic. Customers are led to think that the plaintiff is now the source of such poor quality or undesirable business, goods or services. The goodwill previously attached to the plaintiff's business, goods or services loses its attractive quality and customers are driven away.[485]

III. The Consumer Protection (Fair Trading) Act

440. The Consumer Protection (Fair Trading) Act 2003 (hereinafter 'CPFTA') was enacted to protect consumers against unfair practices and to give them additional rights in respect of goods that do not conform to contract. It allows a consumer who has entered a consumer transaction involving an unfair practice to commence a civil court action against the supplier.[486] An 'unfair practice' arises when a supplier does or says anything, or omits to do or say anything, as a result of which a consumer might reasonably be deceived or misled.[487] An 'unfair practice' also occurs when a supplier makes a false claim in relation to a consumer transaction.[488]

441. An obvious limitation of the CPFTA is that civil action can only be brought by a consumer. Harm caused by ambush marketing is typically to a sponsor, as opposed to a consumer.

442. Section 9 of the CPFTA also allows the court to grant an injunction restraining a supplier from engaging in an unfair practice. The application, however, can only be brought by the Competition and Consumer Commission of Singapore. The utility and efficacy of the provisions of the CPFTA to a sponsor or an event organiser attempting to stop ambush marketing is therefore not high.

---

484. *Ibid.*, at para. 97.
485. *Ibid.*, at para. 98.
486. CPFTA, s. 6.
487. *Ibid.*, s. 4(a).
488. *Ibid.*, s. 4(b).

Chapter 4. Merchandising

443. Merchandising for sports is commonplace. It enables a sports organisation or event to generate revenue by entering into licensing agreements for the production and sale of merchandise related to the organisation or event. Merchandising also has the effect of promoting and advertising the organisation or event, potentially leading to increased attendance by fans, greater funding from other sources (such as Government grants) and increased retail spending on more merchandise. In an August 2023 report, Transparency Market Research noted that the global market for licensed sports merchandise market stood at USD 35.7 billion in 2022 and predicted it to climb to USD 63.7 billion by end-2031.[489]

444. The effective protection of merchandising rights is therefore important. This is typically done by enforcing intellectual property rights, which comprises copyright, trade mark rights, patent rights and design rights. In the sports context, the more important intellectual property rights are trade mark rights and copyright.

445. While civil actions may be brought against parties who infringe intellectual property rights, the question remains as to the practicality of such a measure where the intellectual property rights relate to a sports event. Such events typically do not last more than a few weeks or a month. Although an injunction could be applied for and obtained before or during the event, proceedings to assess damages would likely continue past the end of the event. The applicant would also have to consider the legal costs involved.

§1. Trade Marks

446. In Singapore, protection is accorded to trade marks that are registered under the TMA. The register is maintained by IPOS.

447. A person who does not register his trade mark can continue to use his trade mark in relation to his goods or services but will not be accorded protection under the TMA. Nevertheless, protection may potentially be accorded under the tort of passing off if the elements for the tort can be proven.[490]

448. Section 2(1) of the TMA defines a trade mark as 'any sign capable of being represented graphically and which is capable of distinguishing goods or services dealt with or provided in the course of trade by a person from goods or services so dealt with or provided by any other person'. The TMA is inclusive, in the sense that all marks that fall within the section 2(1) definition are prima facie registrable, unless they fall within the section 7 absolute grounds for the refusal of registration,

489. Transparency Market Research, *Licensed Sports Merchandise Market Outlook 2031*, https://www.transparencymarketresearch.com/licensed-sports-merchandise.html (accessed 23 Nov. 2023).
490. Namely, goodwill, misrepresentation and damages. *See* Part IV, Chapter 3, §4(II) of this text.

or within the section 8 relative grounds for the refusal of registration. The application must also state that (a) the trade mark is being used in the course of trade, by the applicant or with his consent, in relation to those goods or services or (b) the applicant has a bona fide intention that the trade mark should be so used.[491]

449. It is for the Registrar to determine whether a mark is registrable.[492] If the requirements for registration are not met, or if additional information or evidence is required to meet those requirements, the Registrar is obliged to give the applicant an opportunity to make representations, amend the application or furnish the additional or any other information or evidence.[493]

450. Where the Registrar accepts an application for registration, the application will be published in the *Trade Marks* Journal.[494] Any person may oppose the registration within two months after the date of publication of the application for registration.[495] If no notice of opposition is received, or if any opposition proceedings are withdrawn or decided in favour of the applicant, the trade mark will be registered as at the date of the application for registration.[496]

451. The duration of protection for registered trade marks is ten years from the date of registration.[497] Registration may be renewed for further ten-year periods.[498]

452. Cases where notices of opposition were filed in relation to an application to register a sports organisation's trade mark have occurred in Singapore. In *Superbowl Golf School & Country Club Pte Ltd v. National Football League Properties Inc* [2007] SGIPOS 14, the applicant (Superbowl Golf School) applied to register a mark comprising the words 'Superbowl Golf School' for the provision of golf lessons. The opponent (National Football League) opposed the registration of the mark on the grounds that it held the registration of the mark 'Super Bowl' in Singapore and in several countries. The 'Super Bowl' American football games have been held annually since 1967 and have been broadcast in Singapore since 1984. The opponent submitted that there was a likelihood that the public would be confused or deceived that there was a connection between the opponent and applicant if the applicant's application for registration was allowed. IPOS held that the fundamental question is whether, at the date of the application (namely, 17 August 1995), there was a reputation in the opponent's trade marks in Singapore that gave rise to confusion or deception. If the answer was no, then the enquiry stopped there. If the answer was yes, then it would be useful to consider evidence up to the time of opposition for a reality check under more current circumstances. For the present case,

491. TMA, s. 5(2)(e).
492. *Ibid.*, s. 12(1).
493. *Ibid.*, s. 12(3).
494. *Ibid.*, s. 13(1) read with Rule 26(1) of the Trade Marks Rules.
495. Trade Marks Rules, r. 29(1).
496. TMA, s. 15.
497. *Ibid.*, s. 18(1).
498. *Ibid.*, s. 18(2).

IPOS held that there was no real tangible danger of confusion: the opponent's reputation in Singapore was limited, the marks were worded differently and the opponent's goods bore no similarity or association with the applicant's services. The opposition was therefore dismissed, and the registration of the mark was allowed.

453. In *Formula One Licensing BV v. Idea Marketing SA* [2015] 5 SLR 1349, the appellant managed the trade marks for the FIA Formula One World Championship. The respondent was the global promoter for the F1 Powerboat World Championship. On 11 January 2007, the respondent applied to register the mark 'F1H20'. The opposition was dismissed by IPOS. An appeal was filed to the Singapore High Court, which dismissed the appeal and upheld the registration of the mark. The appellant had sought to rely on three marks registered before the application date and one unregistered mark. The court held that the unregistered mark could not be used to oppose the application mark pursuant to section 8(2) of the TMA. As for the three registered marks, the application mark was visually, aurally and conceptually dissimilar from each of the three registered marks, and the appellant could not show a likelihood of confusion. Even if the application mark was similar to any of the registered marks, such similarity was only very slight. Given the conceptual disparity between the application mark and the appellant's marks, the reasonable consumer was unlikely to be confused. Without more evidence, the possibility of confusion was also speculative.

454. In *Polo/Lauren Co LP v. United States Polo Association* [2016] 2 SLR 667, the defendant is the governing body of the sport of polo in the United States and was established in 1890. It applied to register a mark that comprised a graphical representation of two overlapping polo players on horseback, with both holding mallets, next to the text 'USPA'. The plaintiff (a fashion retail company) held a registered mark that featured a graphical representation of one polo player on a horse, raising a mallet. IPOS dismissed the plaintiff's opposition, and the plaintiff appealed the decision. The Singapore High Court dismissed the appeal. It held that there was only an extremely low degree of visual similarity between the application mark and the opposition mark. There was no aural similarity between the application mark and the opposition mark. Even if the opposition mark were pronounced as 'polo player', the reasonable consumer would choose to pronounce the application mark as 'USPA' rather than 'polo players'. There was therefore no likelihood of confusion on the part of the public.

455. In another case featuring the same plaintiff – *The Polo/Lauren Company, L.P. v. Royal County of Berkshire Polo Club Ltd* [2017] SGIPOS 19 – the defendant is a polo club founded in 1985 in the County of Berkshire, England. It applied to register a mark that featured a silhouette of a polo player raising a mallet while on horseback, above the words 'Royal County of Berkshire', which in turn were above the words 'Polo Club'. The mark was registered on 20 October 2011. On 30 December 2013, the plaintiff applied under section 23 of the TMA for the application mark to be declared invalid. IPOS held that the words in the application mark played an essential part in the overall impression conveyed by the mark. The application mark was visually, aurally and conceptually more dissimilar than similar to the plaintiff's registered marks. No likelihood of confusion would arise. IPOS therefore dismissed the invalidation application.

456. Registration of a trade mark confers on its proprietor the exclusive rights to use the trade mark and to authorise other persons to use the trade mark, in relation to the goods or services for which the trade mark is registered.[499] For example, the proprietor can license the use of the trade mark to another party or can sell the trade mark for a sum of money.

457. Infringement of a registered trade mark is actionable by the proprietor of the trade mark.[500] Types of relief that the court may grant include an injunction, damages and account of profits.[501] If the infringement involves the use of a counterfeit trade mark in relation to goods or services, statutory damages may be awarded instead of damages and account of profits.[502] Statutory damages are defined as damages (a) not exceeding SGD 100,000 for each type of goods or service in relation to which the counterfeit trade mark has been used; and (b) not exceeding in the aggregate SGD 1 million, unless the plaintiff proves that his actual loss from such infringement exceeds SGD 1 million. The remedies of damages, account of profits and statutory damages are mutually exclusive, but if damages were ordered, then an account of any profits attributable to the infringement that have not been taken into account in computing the damages may also be awarded.[503]

458. In addition to the remedies of injunction, damages, account of profits and/or statutory damages, the court may also order the infringing person to remove the offending sign from any goods or articles in his possession or to destroy the infringing goods or articles.[504] Furthermore, the court may order that the infringing goods or articles be delivered to the plaintiff for their destruction.[505]

459. The TMA also sets out offences, which have penal consequences. These include:

- counterfeiting a trade mark: section 46;
- falsely applying a registered trade mark to goods or services: section 47;
- making or possessing an article specifically designed or adapted for making copies of a registered trade mark or a sign likely to be mistaken for that trade mark: section 48;
- importing, selling or possessing any goods to which a registered trade mark is falsely applied: section 49;

499. *Ibid.*, s. 26(1).
500. *Ibid.*, s. 31(1).
501. *Ibid.*, s. 31(2).
502. *Ibid.*, s. 31(5).
503. *Ibid.*, s. 31(4).
504. *Ibid.*, s. 32(1).
505. *Ibid.*, ss 33 and 34.

- making a false entry in the Registry of Trade Marks: section 50; and
- falsely representing that a mark is a registered trade mark: section 51.

460. Punishment for these offences includes fines and/or imprisonment. In addition, upon conviction, the court may order forfeiture of the infringing goods or articles.[506]

461. As at the date of writing, there is no reported criminal case that involves the infringement of a sports event's or sports organisation's trade mark. There are, however, reported criminal cases involving the infringement of trade marks held by sportswear brands.[507] In determining the appropriate sentence to be imposed, the court is entitled to take into account all the circumstances in which the offences were committed, including the nature and extent of the infringements and the manner in which the infringements were carried out.[508] Sentencing factors that are typically considered by the court include the following:[509]

- the quantity of the counterfeit goods;
- the value of the items;
- the duration of the infringement;
- whether a syndicate is involved;
- the level of involvement of the offender;
- whether compensation was made;
- whether the infringement was part of the offender's business strategy.

§2. Copyright

462. The Copyright Act 2021 (hereinafter 'Copyright Act') came into force on 21 November 2001. It repealed and replaced the Copyright Act (Chapter 63 of the 2006 Revised Edition). The Copyright Act 2021 factors in technological developments that impact how content is created, distributed, accessed and used.[510]

463. The Copyright Act accords copyright protection to authorial works, which are defined as literary, dramatic, musical and artistic works.[511] Protection is also granted to published editions of authorial works, sound recordings, films, television broadcasts, sound broadcasts, cable programmes, and performances.[512]

506. *Ibid.*, s. 53.
507. Including *Public Prosecutor v. Lin Dunai* [2009] SGDC 328; *Public Prosecutor v. Wang Zhenfu* [2016] SGDC 213; *Public Prosecutor v. Mohd Yusairi Bin Sulaiman* [2010] SGDC 431; and *Public Prosecutor v. Goh Chor Guan* [2010] SGDC 336.
508. *Oh Cheng Hai v. Ong Yong Yew* [1993] 3 SLR(R) 257, at para. 29.
509. *Sentencing Practice in the Subordinate Courts Volume II* (LexisNexis 3rd ed. 2013), p. 1442.
510. Ministry of Law (19 Nov. 2021), *Commencement of the Copyright Act*, https://www.mlaw.gov.sg/news/press-releases/2021-11-19-commencement-of-copyright-act/ (accessed 23 Nov. 2023).
511. Copyright Act, ss 8(a) and 9.
512. *Ibid.*, ss 8(b) to 8(f) and 28.

464. Copyright is an automatic right. Registration is not required.

465. Copyright protection is accorded if the work or the author has some nexus to Singapore. This can be established where the author or maker of the work is a Singapore citizen, Singapore resident, or a body corporate incorporated in Singapore.[513] Nexus to Singapore can also be established if the work or subject matter was made or first published in Singapore, or by or under the direction or control of the Government of Singapore.

466. Copyright protection under the Copyright Act also extends to countries designated as 'reciprocating countries'.[514] Reciprocating countries are countries that are party to the Berne Convention for the Protection of Literary and Artistic Works, or a member of the World Trade Organisation.[515]

467. Under the Copyright Act, content creators are the default copyright owners, including for all types of commissioned content.[516] However, for employee-created content, the employer is the default copyright owner.[517] Parties can agree in writing to reverse the default position.[518]

468. The owner of copyright has certain exclusive rights to control the use and commercial exploitation of the work, such as the exclusive right to reproduce the work, publish the work, perform the work in public, communicate the work to the public, and make an adaptation of the work.[519]

469. The duration of protection depends on factors such as (a) the type of work or subject matter, (b) when the work or subject matter was first published or made, (c) in the case of authorial works, whether the author is identified and if so, when the author is identified, and (d) in the case of authorial works, whether the work was made or first published under the direction or control of the Government of Singapore.[520] Broadly, the duration of protection ranges from twenty-five to seventy years after first publication or making of the work or subject matter.

470. Copyright is infringed if a person does, or authorises the doing of, any act comprised in the copyright, when the person is not the copyright owner and does not have a valid licence from the copyright owner.[521] Copyright can also be infringed when a person deals commercially in an article, the making of which infringed the owner's copyright or was without the copyright owner's consent.[522]

513. *Ibid.*, ss 77 and 78.
514. *Ibid.*, s. 3.
515. Copyright Regulations 2021, r. 6(1).
516. Copyright Act, s. 133.
517. *Ibid.*, s. 134.
518. *Ibid.*, ss 133(3) and 134(5).
519. *Ibid.*, ss 112, 113, 118, 121, 124, 127, and 131.
520. *Ibid.*, ss 114, 115, 119, 122, 125, 128, 129, and 132.
521. *Ibid.*, s. 146.
522. *Ibid.*, ss 147 and 148.

Therefore, copyright owners can take action against a person who knowingly engages in commercial devices with devices that have a limited or no commercially significant purpose besides facilitating access to copyright infringing works. For example, a vendor can be liable for copyright infringement for selling a device, which can connect to a smart television, and which contains pre-loaded applications that can provide viewing access to broadcasted sports events.[523]

471. In order to balance protection of the rights of creators against ensuring that copyright works are reasonably available for the benefit of society at large,[524] the Copyright Act identifies certain exceptions to copyright infringement. Exceptions include:

- Fair use (such as reporting news; criticism or review; research or study).[525]
- Educational use by non-profit educational institutions, under certain conditions.[526]
- Making available accessible-format copies for persons with print disabilities or intellectual disabilities.[527]
- Galleries, libraries, archives and museums making works in their collections available for public use and enjoyment, or research, study or publication (e.g., by making copies, or publicly performing the work).[528]
- For computational data analysis, e.g., sentiment analysis, text and data mining, and training machine learning.[529]

472. The remedies that the Court may grant for a rights infringement may include (a) an injunction; (b) damages, an account of profits, or statutory damages;[530] (c) an order for the infringing party to deliver up infringing material to the owner; and (d) an order for the infringing party to dispose of infringing material.[531]

473. The Copyright Act also sets out various activities that amount to offences. These include:

- Making an article for sale or hire; dealing commercially in an article; importing an article for the purpose of commercial dealing; or possessing an article for the purpose of commercial dealing, when the person doing the act knows or ought reasonably to know that the article is an infringing copy of copyright work.[532]

---

523. Extrapolated from Intellectual Property Office of Singapore (24 Nov. 2022), *Factsheet on Copyright Act 2021*, Illustration on p. 7.
524. Intellectual Property Office of Singapore (24 Nov. 2022), *Factsheet on Copyright Act 2021*, p. 9.
525. Copyright Act, ss 190 to 194.
526. *Ibid.*, ss 195 to 205.
527. *Ibid.*, ss 206 to 220.
528. *Ibid.*, ss 221 to 236.
529. *Ibid.*, ss 243 to 244.
530. As defined at Copyright Act, s. 308.
531. Copyright Act, ss 305, 309 and 310.
532. *Ibid.*, s. 444.

- Wilfully committing a rights infringement, whether or not for commercial advantage.[533]
- Making or possessing an article specifically designed or adapted for making infringing copies of copyright work.[534]
- Distributing or importing or possessing an article, other than for the purposes of trade, to an extent that will prejudicially affect the copyright owner.[535]

474. Punishment for these offences includes fines and/or imprisonment. Sentencing factors that are typically considered by the court include the following:[536]

- the quantity of the infringing copies;
- the value of the infringing copies;
- the level of sophistication of the operation;
- whether a syndicate is involved;
- whether compensation was made to the copyright owner;
- whether the infringement was part of the offender's business strategy.

475. Whether or not a person charged with the offence is convicted, the court may order destruction, or delivery up to the owner, of the infringing copies.[537]

476. If there is reasonable cause to suspect that an item, located at any premises, is evidence of an offence having been committed, the Court may issue a warrant authorising a police officer to enter and search the premises for the item, and to seize such item if found.[538]

477. As at the date of writing, there is no reported criminal case that involves the infringement of a sports event's or sports organisation's copyright.

§3. Passing Off

478. The law regarding the tort of passing off has been covered in Part IV, Chapter 3, §4 II of this text and will not be repeated.

479. In terms of case law, *The Singapore Professional Golfers' Association v. Chen Eng Waye and Others* [2013] 2 SLR 495 involved the bringing of a passing-off action by a sports association against another sports association and its partners. The plaintiff was a non-profit golfing association registered under the Societies Act. Its initials were 'SPGA' and its shortened name was 'Singapore PGA'. Its objectives included promoting the sports of golf in Singapore and the interests of its professional golfer members. The third defendant was named 'Singapore Senior PGA

533. *Ibid.*, ss 445 and 449.
534. *Ibid.*, s. 446.
535. *Ibid.*, s. 448.
536. *Sentencing Practice in the Subordinate Courts Volume II* (LexisNexis 3rd ed. 2013), p. 1428.
537. Copyright Act, s. 455.
538. *Ibid.*, s. 456.

LLP' and its initials were 'SSPGA'. The partners of the third defendant were the first defendant and his son the second defendant. The third defendant was set up after the first defendant's membership with the plaintiff was terminated.

480. In January 2011, the third defendant advertised that it would conduct a Senior Professional Qualifying Test in March 2011 exclusively for senior golfers. In February 2011, the plaintiff also announced that it would conduct a test for golfers aged 50 and above to qualify as senior professional golfers. The plaintiff eventually commenced a suit against the defendants for the tort of passing off. The trial judge held that the plaintiff could not establish any misrepresentation and dismissed the claim. On appeal, the Singapore Court of Appeal allowed the appeal against the first and third defendants, but dismissed the appeal against the second defendant. The following principles as stated by the Court of Appeal are instructive:

(a) Although the tort of passing off is most often associated with the goodwill of traders, the protection it confers can and does extend to non-commercial organisations. Such associations typically benefit from and depend upon voluntary membership, subscriptions, donations or support. Such support reflected the magnetic force of the particular association in question, and this constitutes goodwill which could be damaged by a misrepresentation that amounts to passing off: at [23].[539]
(b) Regarding the element of misrepresentation, the key enquiry was whether the relevant public would likely be led to believe that the goods, services or activities offered by the defendant were those of the claimant, or of an entity connected to or associated with the plaintiff. The relevant segment of the public would consist of all those persons who had an actual or potential interest, whether directly or indirectly, in the plaintiff's products, services or activities. In this case, the relevant segment of the public could include any person with a commercial interest in golf as well as those who had or intended to have either direct or indirect dealings with the plaintiff in relation to its purposes, objects and/or activities: at [49] and [50].
(c) Loss arising from damage to goodwill in relation to non-commercial associations, such as the plaintiff, would include a loss of actual or prospective members and, therefore, a loss of subscriptions or other income derived from membership: at [66].
(d) Furthermore, the plaintiff relied on sponsorships to run its activities and to keep itself in operation. The third defendant also intended to rely on sponsorships to fund its activities such as golf tournaments. The amount of sponsorship funding is finite, and if the relevant segment of the public perceived mistakenly that the two parties were related, it would be easy to see a real prospect that sponsorship and funding meant for the plaintiff might be diverted to support the activities of the third defendant: at [67].

---

539. The Court of Appeal cited Christopher Wadlow, *The Law of Passing-Off: Unfair Competition by Misrepresentation* (Sweet & Maxwell 4th ed. 2011), at paras 3-022 and 3-042.

(e) There was a real likelihood that senior golfers might obtain their qualification from the third defendant instead of from the plaintiff as long as the golfing public, especially aspiring senior professional golfers, think that accreditation with either body is equivalent for all purposes because of the perceived connection between the plaintiff and the third defendant. This would cause the plaintiff to lose income from test administration and certification fees: at [68].

Chapter 5. Betting and Gambling

481. On 14 February 2022, the Gambling Control Bill and Gambling Regulatory Authority of Singapore Bill were first read in Parliament. Both Bills were passed and came into effect on 1 August 2022.

482. The GCA consolidated the law on the suppression of various forms of unlawful gambling and the regulation of authorised gambling services outside of casinos; and repealed the Betting Act 1960, the Common Gaming Houses Act 1961, the Private Lotteries Act 2011 and the Remote Gambling Act 2014.

483. The Casino Control Act 2006, which regulates gaming in casinos, remains in place. Where a gambling syndicate is involved, provisions of the OCA may also be triggered.

484. The Gambling Regulatory Authority of Singapore Act 2022 (hereinafter 'GRA Act') established the Gambling Regulatory Authority (hereinafter 'GRA') (formerly known as the Casino Regulatory Authority of Singapore) to oversee regulation of all forms of gambling in Singapore. Previously, the regulation of different forms of gambling had been overseen by multiple Government entities.

485. Sports betting is permitted only where the operator is granted a licence by the GRA. At the date of writing, Singapore Pools (Private) Limited (hereinafter 'Singapore Pools') is the only gambling operator authorised to offer sports betting services. Singapore Pools is a wholly owned subsidiary of the Singapore Totalisator Board (commonly known as the 'Tote Board'). The Tote Board is a statutory board under the Ministry of Finance. The Tote Board is allowed to collect bets on only three types of sports events: horse racing, football matches and Formula 1 races.[540]

486. Singapore Pools is a member of the United Lotteries for Integrity in Sports (hereinafter 'ULIS'), which is an international association of state lotteries. ULIS provides stakeholders with a global sports betting monitoring system in order to detect suspicious betting patterns.[541] ULIS's objectives include:[542]

– Monitoring and sharing information about suspicious betting patterns or other practices that could indicate a breach of sports integrity.
– Supporting investigations with evidence of suspicious betting patterns.

540. GCA, Second Schedule, Parts 2, 4 and 6; read with Betting (Exemption) Notification 2009 and Betting (Singapore Totalisator Board – Exemption) Notification 2019.
Prior to 7 Jan. 2019, football and Formula one bets were placed with Singapore Pools, whereas horse racing bets were placed with the Singapore Turf Club, which is part of the Tote Board Group. With effect from 7 Jan. 2019, Singapore Pools took over the betting operations and outlets of the Singapore Turf Club.

541. United Lotteries for Integrity in Sports, *About ULIS*, https://ulis.org/about-ulis (accessed 24 Nov. 2023).

542. United Lotteries for Integrity in Sports, *What We Do*, https://ulis.org/what-we-do (accessed 24 Nov. 2023).

- Cooperating with law enforcement agencies, betting regulators and sports organisations on exchanging information related to sports integrity issues.
- Developing and implementing educational resources and programs for preventing competition manipulation, illegal betting practices, and fighting against crime in sports.
- Keeping members up to date by regularly sharing best practices and case studies.

487. Aside from sports betting, gambling may also take place at the premises of sports clubs, for example through jackpot machines installed at clubs as an alternative means of earning revenue for the club. Clubs in Singapore are allowed to operate jackpot machines (also known as fruit machines) if they are granted the requisite licence to operate a gaming machine room by the GRA under section 54 of the GCA.

§1. Gaming Control Act 2022

488. The GCA defines 'gambling' to include:[543]

- Betting: this term is defined as 'making or accepting a bet, involving payment or staking of any money or money equivalent or anything else of value on (a) the outcome of an event or process, taking place in Singapore or elsewhere; (b) the likelihood of anything occurring or not occurring, in Singapore or elsewhere; or (c) whether anything is or is not true'.[544] 'Betting' may be deemed to take place even if the event or process betted upon has already occurred and one party to the transaction knows the outcome.[545]
- Engaging in gaming activity: this term is defined as (a) playing a game of chance for a prize, or (b) playing a gaming machine (such as a jackpot machine or fruit machine[546]).[547] A 'game of chance for a prize' is played where a person plays a game of chance and thereby acquires a chance of winning any money or money equivalent or anything else of value.[548] A 'game of chance' includes games with elements of both chance and skill, games where the element of chance can be eliminated by superlative skill; and games that are presented as involving an element of chance.[549]
- Participating in lotteries: this term refers to (a) participating in an arrangement, scheme, competition or device; (b) there may be one or multiple participants; (c) entitlement to participate depends on provision of money or money equivalent or anything else of value, or merely on the participant's attendance without payment; (d) the outcome is the distribution of prizes; and (e) the distribution

543. GCA, s. 4.
544. *Ibid.*, s. 5(1).
545. *Ibid.*, s. 5(4).
546. *Ibid.*, s. 7(6), Illustration.
547. GCA, s. 7(1).
548. *Ibid.*, s. 7(2).
549. *Ibid.*, s. 7(6).

depends on an element of chance, whether or not an element of skill is also involved. Specific examples set out in the GCA include 'lucky draws, raffles and sweepstakes'.[550]

489. The definition of 'gambling' is plainly wide. Nevertheless, the GCA carves out exceptions for activities such as:

– any business agreement entered into between parties, the making or performance of which by any party constitutes an investment activity;[551]
– playing an amusement machine, which is operated by inserting money or money equivalent or gaming token or use of credits, where any individual playing the machine once receives nothing, or an item of value of less than SGD 100, or an opportunity to play again without paying further. An example of such a machine is a claw machine;[552]
– social gambling: this is defined as non-remote gambling that is conducted in a person's home, amongst family members or persons who know each other personally, is substantially spontaneous (even if it occurs habitually or arrangement), and is not promoted for business or by a third party.[553]

490. The definition of 'gambling' and the conduct of gambling, as defined in the GCA, is technology-neutral. For example, section 6(3)(b) of the GCA states that a reference in the GCA to a bet made with, or received by, a betting operator includes a bet made with the betting operator wholly or partly by means of remote communication. A 'betting exchange' is defined to mean 'a facility, electronic or otherwise' that enables persons to place or accept bets.[554]

491. Gaming offences are set out in Part 2 of the GCA. These include conducting gambling without a licence or approval from the GRA, conducting gambling in a venue that is not an approved gambling venue, gambling with an unlicensed gambling service provider, having a financial interest in a gambling service, owning a place used for unlawful gambling, organising or managing an unlawful gambling place, providing financing in order to organise or conduct an unlawful gambling place, being in an unlawful gambling place, supplying prohibited or unapproved gaming machines, and using prohibited or unapproved gaming machines (whether in-person or by proxy).

492. Penalties include fines and/or imprisonment terms. The penalty structure is three-tiered, differentiating between operators who set up the unlawful gambling activity, agents who facilitate the conduct of the activity, and punters who participate in the activity. The highest penalties are imposed on operators, followed by agents, and then punters.

550. *Ibid.*, s. 9(1).
551. *Ibid.*, s. 5(2).
552. *Ibid.*, s. 7(6).
553. *Ibid.*, s. 12.
554. *Ibid.*, s. 6(6).

493. The minimum age for gambling at Singapore Pools' physical outlets is 18. The minimum age for gambling in all other situations is 21.[555] Section 31 of the GCA criminalises underaged gambling, on a strict liability basis.[556] Section 32 criminalises a situation where an underaged individual intentionally enters or remains in a gambling venue, or opens an account to engage in remote gambling. In these cases, a convicted individual is liable to a fine.[557]

494. Given the recent introduction of the GCA, there has been no reported case involving offences under the GCA as at the date of writing. Guidance may be provided by past cases involving offences under the Betting Act 1960 and the Remote Gambling Act 2014.

495. The case of *Lim Bee Ngan Karen v. Public Prosecutor* [2015] 4 SLR 1120 *inter alia* involved offences under the Betting Act 1960 for carrying out unlawful betting (which is an offence under section 20 of the GRA). The Singapore High Court noted that factors that the court may take into consideration when considering the sentence to be meted out include whether the Internet was used to perpetuate offences as the Internet provides a shroud of anonymity that makes it harder to detect offences,[558] whether the offender is charged with one offence or multiple offences that span a long period of time,[559] and the value of the bets involved.[560] Other factors that may be considered include whether the offences involved a substantial and organised operation with sophisticated and high-technology equipment[561] and the role played by the offender.[562]

496. In *Lau Jian Bang v. Public Prosecutor* [2020] 3 SLR 1161, the Singapore High Court set out a sentencing framework for offences under section 8 of the Remote Gambling Act 2014, which criminalised using a remote gambling service provided by an unlicensed operator (which is an offence under section 20 of the GRA). The Court considered that the harm caused by such an offence is not such that it attracts imprisonment as a matter of course for first-time offenders.[563] The starting point for first-time offenders was a fine,[564] which would then be adjusted to take into account the quantum of the offender's bets, as well as other aggravating or mitigating factors present.[565] The Court was of the view that a custodial sentence should generally only be imposed in the case of repeat offenders.[566]

---

555. *Ibid.*, s. 13.
556. *Ibid.*, s. 31(6).
557. *Ibid.*, ss 31(2) and 32(3).
558. *Lim Bee Ngan Karen v. Public Prosecutor* [2015] 4 SLR 1120, paras 66 and 67.
559. *Ibid.*, para. 69.
560. *Ibid.*, para. 64.
561. *Auyok Kim Tye v. Public Prosecutor* [2001] SGMC 17, para. 18.
562. *Ng Him Moi v. Public Prosecutor* [2015] SGMC 22, para. 26.
563. *Lau Jian Bang v. Public Prosecutor* [2020] 3 SLR 1161, at para. 51.
564. *Ibid.*, at para. 60.
565. *Ibid.*, at paras 62 and 63.
566. *Ibid.*, at para. 64.

497. In *Koo Kah Yee v. Public Prosecutor* [2020] SGHC 261, the Honourable the Chief Justice of Singapore sitting in his appellate capacity in the Singapore High Court set out a sentencing framework for offences under section 11(1) of the Remote Gambling Act 2014, which criminalised providing a Singapore-based remote gambling service (which is an offence under section 18 of the GRA). The sentencing considerations are broadly divided into offence-specific factors and offender-specific factors.[567]

498. In terms of offence-specific factors, the court should generally consider (a) the degree of harm caused by the offence; and (b) the degree of the offender's culpability. Offence-specific factors going towards harm include the aggregate value of bets involved, whether a syndicate is involved, whether there is a transnational element, and the difficulty of detection. Offence-specific factors going towards culpability include the degree of planning and premeditation, level of sophistication, the offender's role, the offender's personal gain, and the duration of offending.[568]

499. Offender-specific factors are namely aggravating factors (such as the offender's relevant antecedents, or evident lack of remorse) and mitigating factors (such as a guilty plea or cooperation with the authorities).[569]

500. Where a person is convicted of an offence under the GCA, the Court may – in addition to the sentence imposed – order forfeiture of (a) any item used in the commission of the offence, (b) any money or money equivalent or other thing of value used in the commission of the offence, or (c) the winnings or reward obtained by the convicted person from the commission of the offence.[570]

501. Separately, an argument that the *de minimis* principle set out in section 95 of the Penal Code is applicable to offences under the GCA may not carry any weight. Section 95 of the Penal Code states:

> **Act causing slight harm**
>
> **95.** Nothing is an offence by reason that it causes, or that it is intended to cause, or that it is known to be likely to cause, any harm, if that harm is so slight that no person of ordinary sense and temper would complain of such harm.

502. In *Aw Sei Kui v. Public Prosecutor* [1998] 2 SLR(R) 64 at [50], the Singapore High Court held that it is implicit in the wording of section 95 that the harm referred to must mean physical, mental, psychological or economic harm suffered by an individual. Harm caused by an offence against society, such as gambling or drug-related offences, or minor breaches of road traffic regulations is not susceptible to

567. *Koo Kah Yee v. Public Prosecutor* [2020] SGHC 261, at para. 54.
568. *Ibid.*, at para. 55.
569. *Ibid.*, at para. 66.
570. GCA, ss 40–41.

measurement. The actual harm done by such an offence may be insignificant, but that fact would not qualify the offender as exempt from punishment under the *de minimis* principle. The cumulative effect of many slight offences causes great harm to society as a whole, and therefore meaning can only be given to the law if it blankets the entire range of offenders.

503. The GCA contains special provisions relating to remote gambling. Under section 117, an access blocking order may be served on an internet service provider to disable access to an online location providing a remote gambling service. Pursuant to section 118, if a person has participated in unlawful remote gambling activity, a financial institution or a financial transaction provider may be issued with a payment blocking order. The payment blocking order can include ordering the financial institution or a financial transaction provider not to accept credit extended to the individual, not to accept any cheque or similar instrument in favour of the individual, not to accept any electronic funds transfer to or from that person, and to block payments using merchant category codes customarily associated with gambling transactions.

504. In November 2022, it was reported that the GRA had by then blocked about 1,200 remote gambling websites, about 250 bank accounts, and payments of more than SGD 33 million linked to remote gambling services.[571]

§2. ORGANISED CRIME ACT 2015

505. The Organised Crime Bill was introduced in Parliament in July 2015. During the Second Reading of the Bill, the Minister for Home Affairs explained that organised crime groups are typically well resourced and able to mount and sustain large-scale illegal activities over prolonged periods. Such groups are often international and have a many-layered structure. The Bill, therefore, sought to 'enhance [Singapore's] ability to disrupt the activities of organised crime groups at various levels of their hierarchy so as to prevent them from establishing a foothold to perpetrate serious crimes'.[572]

506. Section 2(1) of the OCA defines an organised criminal group as a group that has as one of its objectives the obtaining of a financial or other material or financial benefits from the facilitation or commission of any person of any serious offence (whether occurring inside or outside Singapore). The types of 'serious offence' are set out in the Schedule of the OCA and include a majority of the offences under Part 2 of the GCA.

571. Ministry of Home Affairs (17 Nov. 2022), *Joint Efforts to Tackle Unlawful and Problem Gambling During World Cup 2022*, https://www.mha.gov.sg/mediaroom/press-releases/joint-efforts-to-tackle-unlawful-and-problem-gambling-during-world-cup-2022 (accessed 29 Nov. 2023).

572. Mr S Iswaran (17 Aug. 2015), *Singapore Parliamentary Report,* vol. 93, sitting no. 22 page 30, available at https://sprs.parl.gov.sg/search/#/sprs3topic?reportid=bill-151 (accessed 9 Jan. 2019).

507. Offences in the OCA include the following:

- being a member of a locally-linked organised criminal group: section 5;
- recruiting members for an organised criminal group (whether within or outside Singapore): section 6;
- directly or indirectly instructing another person to commit an offence for an organised criminal group (whether within or outside Singapore): section 7;
- procuring (whether from one's own self or from any other person) any expenditure or use of property in support of, or to aid or promote the commission of, an offence for an organised criminal group: sections 8 and 9;
- allowing an organised criminal group to use premises owned or occupied by the accused to support, aid or promote the commission of an offence: section 10;
- dealing with property illegally obtained by an organised crime group, or used by an organised crime group to commit an offence: section 11;
- facilitating the commission of an offence for an organised criminal group: section 12; and
- committing an offence under any written law of Singapore for an organised criminal group: section 13.

508. The offences set out in sections 6 to 13 of the OCA may be committed by a person inside or outside Singapore.

509. The OCA further provides for the issuance of Preventive Orders (namely, the Organised Crime Prevention Order, the Financial Reporting Order and the Disqualification Order) and a civil confiscation regime.[573] Since applications can be made via civil proceedings, the application can proceed even where a person is not charged or is acquitted.

510. The OCA was first invoked in November 2017 against six persons allegedly involved in a gambling syndicate that had amassed more than SGD 25 million in illicit proceeds. The first conviction under the OCA was secured when one of the six persons pleaded guilty in June 2018 to various gambling and organised crime offences. His total sentence was two years' imprisonment and a fine of SGD 50,000.[574]

§3. Confiscation Orders

511. Pursuant to section 7 of the CDSA, where a person has been convicted of one or more 'serious offences', the Public Prosecutor can apply for a confiscation order in respect of benefits derived by the person from his criminal conduct. The list of 'serious offences' is set out in the Second Schedule of the CDSA and includes

573. OCA, Parts 3 to 7 and 9.
574. Jalelah Abu Baker (27 Jun. 2018), *Member of Remote Gambling Syndicate Sentenced to 2 Years' Jail, Fined S$50,000*, Channel NewsAsia, https://www.channelnewsasia.com/news/singapore/member-of-remote-gambling-syndicate-sentenced-to-2-years-jail-10474970 (accessed 9 Jan. 2019).

all of the offences under Part 2 of the GCA (save for those offences committed by underaged individuals), as well as several provisions in the OCA.

512. For example, on 15 January 2019, a couple who had been convicted for gambling-related offences were ordered to pay SGD 1,122,916.73 to the Government pursuant to a confiscation order made under the CDSA. In a statement released by the Singapore Police Force, it was stated that the couple had 'accumulated an unexplained wealth … disproportionate to their known sources of income'.[575]

513. In another example, a man was convicted and sentenced on 16 February 2017 under the Betting Act 1960 for intentionally aiding another to act as a bookmaker to accept bets. The bookmaker had shared the winnings and losses from the bets with the offender. Investigations uncovered that the offender accumulated unexplained wealth of SGD 258,666.14 from 2012 to 2014. Following the offender's conviction, this sum was assessed to be benefits that he derived from gambling-related offences, and a confiscation order was made.[576]

514. If a civil confiscation order is obtained against a person under the OCA, a confiscation order under section 5 of the CDSA may also be made in addition to the OCA confiscation order: section 8 of the CDSA.

§4. Jackpot Machines

515. Clubs in Singapore may operate jackpot machines (also known as fruit machines) if they are granted the requisite permit under section 54 of the GRA. It was reported in July 2017 that at the time, eighty-two clubs were operating close to 1,900 jackpot machines across Singapore.[577] The clubs included football clubhouses.

516. In October 2016, the chairman of a local football club stated during an interview with the press that the use of jackpot machines to earn revenue for the club was 'the best available model for the time being'.[578] In April 2017, it was reported that the football club had announced that its gross income for the financial year ending in March 2016 was SGD 36.8 million, which was more than the SGD

575. Singapore Police Force (17 Jan. 2019), *Confiscation of Unexplained Wealth from Two Illegal Gambling Agents*, https://www.police.gov.sg/media-room/news/20190117_confiscation_of_unexplained_wealth_from_two_illegal_gambling_agents_others (accessed 18 Jan. 2019).

576. Singapore Police Force (26 Aug. 2019), *Confiscation Order Made Against Illegal Soccer Betting Bookmaker For Benefits Derived From Criminal Conduct*, https://www.police.gov.sg/media-room/news/20190826_arrest_confiscation_order_made_against_illegal_soccer_betting_bookmaker_cad (accessed 26 Mar. 2021).

577. Bei Yi, Seow (20 Jul. 2017), *Tighter Regulations for Clubs with Jackpot Machines to Guard Against Problem Gambling*, The Straits Times, https://www.straitstimes.com/singapore/tighter-regulations-for-clubs-with-jackpot-machines-to-guard-against-problem-gambling (accessed 5 Mar. 2019).

578. Shamir Osman (19 Oct. 2016), *Jackpot's the Answer*, The New Paper, https://www.tnp.sg/sports/singapore-football/jackpots-answer (accessed 5 Mar. 2019).

35.8 million budget of its NSA the FAS for the same period.[579] On the very same day, SportSG announced that it had lodged a police report *inter alia* over the suspected misuse of the football club's funds.[580]

517. On 20 July 2017, the Ministry of Home Affairs announced changes to the regulation of fruit machines.[581] At the time, a club was allowed to operate fruit machines *inter alia* if it provided at least two other recreational facilities. Due to some clubs relying on fruit machines as a major activity, the Ministry announced tightening of the permit criteria for fruit machines. One ground for assessing future renewals and applications for fruit machine permits would be whether the club provided a suitably wide range of substantive recreational and social facilities and services to their members. The Ministry also announced the tightening of fruit machine quotas, the limiting of the operating hours of fruit machine rooms and the restriction of entry to fruit machine rooms to individuals who hold membership terms of at least one year and are aged at least 21 years old (previously, those aged 18 and above could enter fruit machine rooms). In light of the regulatory changes, local football clubs could no longer operate jackpot machines.[582]

518. As at November 2022, licences to operate gaming machine rooms have been granted to twenty-five social clubs and entities.[583] None of the licensees are football clubs.

579. Meng Meng, Wang (20 Apr. 2017), *Football: Tiong Bahru FC Amassed $37 Million from Jackpot Revenue*, The Straits Times, https://www.straitstimes.com/singapore/football-tiong-bahru-fc-amassed-37-million-from-jackpot-revenue (accessed 5 Mar. 2019).

580. Lin Fhoong, Low (20 Apr. 2017), *High Drama as Police Raid FAS Office, 3 Football Clubs*, Today, https://www.todayonline.com/singapore/police-raid-fas-3-football-clubs-police-report-lodged-against-tiong-bahru-fc (accessed 5 Mar. 2019).

581. Ministry of Home Affairs (20 Jul. 2017), *Changes to Regulation of Fruit Machines*, https://www.mha.gov.sg/mediaroom/press-releases/changes-to-regulation-of-fruit-machines/ (accessed 5 Mar. 2019).

582. Ministry of Culture, Community and Youth (8 Nov. 2022), *Cessation of Jackpot Operations at the Singapore Premier League (SPL) Clubs*, https://www.mccy.gov.sg/about-us/news-and-resources/parliamentary-matters/2022/Nov/cessation-of-jackpot-operations-at-the-singapore-premier-league-spl-clubs (accessed 29 Nov. 2023).

583. Gambling Regulatory Authority, *List of Gaming Machine Room Licensees*, https://www.gra.gov.sg/docs/default-source/default-document-library/list-of-approved-gaming-machine-room-licensees.pdf (accessed 29 Nov. 2023).

COVID-19 and Its Impact on National Sport

519. Since it was first identified in December 2019, coronavirus disease 2019 (known as COVID-19) has affected the entire globe. Millions have been infected with the virus, and many have not survived. The World Health Organization declared the situation as a pandemic on 11 March 2020.[584] In an effort to stem the spread of the virus, several countries have gone into and come out of lockdowns, with some countries going into more than one lockdown. Restrictions on personal liberties under lockdown vary from country to country.

520. As at June 2021, Singapore has experienced one lockdown. What was defined by the Government as a 'circuit breaker' was imposed from 7 April 2020 to 1 June 2020.

521. Prior to the circuit breaker, steps had been taken to reduce local transmission of COVID-19. With effect from 26 March 2020, gatherings were limited to not more than ten persons.[585] All events and mass gatherings (including sporting events) were ordered to be deferred or cancelled, regardless of size.[586] SportSG released an advisory for sports and physical exercise activities, listing best practices, and setting out rules and regulations for gyms, studios, outdoor programmes, stadiums, swimming pools, and indoor sports halls.[587]

522. Measures were subsequently tightened during the circuit breaker period. Except for entities providing essential services, all other workplaces were closed, with staff ordered to work from home.[588] All schools were shifted to full home-based learning.[589] All persons were encouraged to remain largely at home, although

584. World Health Organization (11 Mar. 2020), *WHO Director-General's opening remarks at the media briefing on COVID-19*, https://www.who.int/director-general/speeches/detail/who-director-general-s-opening-remarks-at-the-media-briefing-on-covid-19---11-march-2020 (accessed 3 May 2021).
585. Ministry of Health (24 Mar. 2020), *Tighter Measures to Minimise Further Spread of COVID-19*, https://www.moh.gov.sg/news-highlights/details/tighter-measures-to-minimise-further-spread-of-covid-19, para. 6b (accessed 3 May 2021).
586. *Ibid.*, para. 12 (accessed 3 May 2021).
587. SportSG (25 Mar. 2020), *Advisory for Sport and Physical Exercise Activities*, https://www.sportsingapore.gov.sg/newsroom/media-releases/2020/advisory-for-sport-and-physical-exercise-activities (accessed 3 May 2021).
588. Ministry of Health (3 Apr. 2020), *Circuit Breaker to Minimise Further Spread of COVID-19*, https://www.moh.gov.sg/news-highlights/details/circuit-breaker-to-minimise-further-spread-of-covid-19, paras 4 to 13 (accessed 3 May 2021).
589. *Ibid.*, para. 16 (accessed 3 May 2021).

they could leave home for meals or other essentials, and procure essential services.[590] Sports and recreation facilities, such as public swimming pools, country clubs, gyms and fitness studios, were closed.[591] Although not encouraged, individuals were allowed to leave home to walk, run, cycle or engage in other similar exercises, either alone or only with persons living in the same household.[592]

523. Given the closure of sports facilities, athletes had to devise new home-based training routines by utilising different equipment to maintain their fitness and practice.[593] Student-athletes in the Singapore Sports School had to check in daily with their academy mentors, coaches and teammates, while relying on online training videos and self-discipline to maintain training intensity.[594]

524. On 19 May 2020, the Government announced that with effect from 2 June 2020, Singapore would move out of the circuit breaker and embark on a three-phased approach to resume activities safely.

525. Phase 1 (termed the 'Safe Re-opening' phase) took place from 2 to 18 June 2020. It was reported[595] that thirty athletes who had qualified or were close to qualifying for the 2021 Tokyo Olympic and Paralympic Games were allowed to resume training under controlled conditions at selected venues. Protocols were also put in place. Individuals had to maintain a safe distance, take their temperatures, and observe contact tracing procedures. Those in the training venues had to wear masks when not engaged in strenuous activities, and a maximum of five people, inclusive of coaches and specialists, were allowed in at any time. Some NSAs also implemented their own plans. For example, the Singapore Swimming Association marked out a specific route for athletes to enter and exit the training facility at the Singapore Sports Hub to ensure no interaction between individuals. Swimmers were required to arrive in their swimming costumes and train in alternate lanes and were not allowed to shower at the facility.

---

590. *Ibid.*, para. 14 (accessed 3 May 2021).
591. *Ibid.*, para. 18 (accessed 3 May 2021).
592. SportSG (17 May 2020), *(Updated) Advisory on Tightened Measures for Sport and Physical Exercise During The Extended Circuit Breaker Period* (Till 1 Jun. 2020), https://www.sportsingapore.gov.sg/Newsroom/Media-Releases/2020/(Updated)-Advisory-on-Tightened-Measures-on-Sport-and-Physical-Exercise (accessed 3 May 2021).
593. *On Home Ground: How Singapore Athletes Are Staying Fit and Sharp During Covid-19 Circuit Breaker* (8 May 2020), The Straits Times, https://www.straitstimes.com/sport/on-home-ground-how-singapore-athletes-are-staying-fit-and-sharp-during-covid-19-circuit (accessed 3 May 2021).
594. *Student-Athletes Unbreakable During 'Circuit Breaker'* (April 2020), Singapore Sports School, https://www.sportsschool.edu.sg/news-and-publications/archive/apr20/student-athletes-unbreakable-during-circuit-breaker (accessed 3 May 2021).
595. Kwek, Kimberly (1 Jun. 2020), *Coronavirus: Olympics-Bound TeamSG athletes can Train Again from Tuesday under 'controlled conditions'*, The Straits Times, https://www.straitstimes.com/sport/coronavirus-olympics-bound-teamsg-athletes-can-resume-training-from-tuesday-under-controlled (accessed 3 May 2021).

526. For the general public, however, public and private sports and recreational facilities remained closed.[596] Nevertheless, fitness operators were granted access to their business facilities for the purpose of recording content for online classes involving limited number of staff.[597]

527. Phase 2 (the 'Safe Transition' phase) took place from 19 June 2020 to 27 December 2020. Sports activity, including contact sports, was permitted to resume.[598] Sport and recreational facilities were permitted to reopen but could only admit a maximum number of persons based on the facility's gross floor area (10 square metres per person, and subject to a cap of no more than fifty persons). Group activities were limited to not more than five persons (excluding one instructor or coach). However, restrictions that remained in place included safe distancing measures and the wearing of masks at all times except when performing strenuous exercise.

528. The Singapore Premier League resumed on 17 October 2020.[599] Given that athletes had not been able to maintain match fitness during the circuit breaker and Phase 1, the FAS amended the rules by temporarily increasing the number of substitutions to five (up from three) and introducing two mandatory water breaks per match.[600]

529. Phase 3 (the 'Safe Nation' phase) started on 28 December 2020. Safety measures were further relaxed, but they still remained in place.[601] For example, the maximum number of persons allowed in a sports or recreational facility was increased (8 square metres per person), and the number of persons who engage in group activities increased to eight. Nevertheless, all participants had to observe safe distancing measures and wear masks except when performing strenuous exercise.

---

596. SportSG (24 May 2020), *Advisory On Gradual Resumption of Sport and Physical Exercise/ Activity after Circuit Breaker (2 June Onwards)*, https://www.sportsingapore.gov.sg/Newsroom/Media-Releases/2020/Advisory-On-Gradual-Resumption-Of-Sport-And-Physical-Exercise-and-Activity-After-Circuit-Breaker, para. 2 (accessed 3 May 2021).
597. SportSG (18 Nov. 2020), *Advisory on Gradual Resumption of Sport and Physical Exercise/ Activity after Circuit Breaker (2 June Onwards)*, https://www.sportsingapore.gov.sg/Newsroom/Media-Releases/2020/Advisory-On-Gradual-Resumption-Of-Sport-And-Physical-Exercise-and-Activity-After-Circuit-Breaker, para. 3 (accessed 3 May 2021).
598. SportSG (24 May 2020), *(Updated as of 18 Nov. 2020) Advisory for Resumption of Sport and Physical Exercise and Activity for Phase Two Safe Transition*, https://www.sportsingapore.gov.sg/Newsroom/Media-Releases/2020/Advisory-For-Resumption-Of-Sport-And-Physical-Exercise-and-Activity-For-Phase-Two-Safe-Transition (accessed 3 May 2021).
599. Football Association of Singapore (9 Oct. 2020), *2020 AIA Singapore Premier League Season to Resume on 17 October 2020*, https://www.fas.org.sg/2020-aia-singapore-premier-league-season-to-resume-on-17-october-2020/ (accessed 3 May 2021).
600. Football Association of Singapore (14 Oct. 2020), *Comprehensive Match Protocols Established for 2020 AIA Singapore Premier League Resumption*, https://www.fas.org.sg/comprehensive-match-protocols-established-for-2020-aia-singapore-premier-league-resumption/ (accessed 3 May 2021).
601. SportSG (24 Dec. 2020), *Advisory for Resumption of Sport and Physical Exercise & Activity For Phase Three ('Safe Nation')*, https://www.sportsingapore.gov.sg/Newsroom/Media-Releases/2020/Advisory-For-Resumption-Of-Sport-And-Physical-Exercise-,-a-,-Activity-For-Phase-Three-(%E2%80%9CSafe-Nation%E2%80%9D) (accessed 3 May 2021).

530. Due to an increasing number of COVID-19 cases in the community in early May 2021, the nation entered into Phase 2 (Heightened Alert) with effect from 16 May 2021.[602] A stricter set of measures was put in place for all sports activities. Sport/recreational facilities could only admit a maximum number of persons according to their gross floor area (16 square metres per person, and subject to a cap of no more than fifty persons). Group activities were confined to no more than two individuals. Multiple groups of two carrying out the same activity were allowed subject to safe distancing measures, such as remaining at least 3 metres apart. Participants in all indoor sports activities were required to keep face masks on at all times, thereby limiting indoor activity to low-intensity activity.

531. As at mid-June 2021, Singapore had entered into Phase 3 (Heightened Alert), which came into effect on 14 June 2021.[603] Restrictions, such as on group size and mask-wearing, were relaxed from the Phase 2 (Heightened Alert) rules. A new requirement was announced, namely that instructors and staff who come into contact with unmasked users in the course of their work would be progressively scheduled to undergo regular COVID-19 testing. Live spectator sports events and mass participation sports events were allowed to resume, subject to limitations.

532. Despite the continuing presence of COVID-19 safety measures, the situation in Singapore has been well-managed, to the extent that there has been a level of comfort in opening Singapore up to international events. For example, in February 2021, Singapore hosted the week-long Singapore Tennis Open tournament, which is an ATP 250 indoor hard-court tennis event. Over fifty players from more than fifteen countries competed.[604] Up to two hundred and fifty spectators were allowed to attend per day to watch the semi-final and final matches, subject to pre-event testing for COVID-19.[605]

533. Since the first case of COVID-19 was confirmed in Singapore on 23 January 2020,[606] the Government introduced various financial stimulus packages to

602. SportSG (14 May 2021), *Further Stricter Safe Management Measures for Sport and Physical Exercise & Activity* (16 May To 13 Jun. 2021), https://www.sportsingapore.gov.sg/Newsroom/Media-Releases/2021/May/Further-Stricter-Safe-Management-Measures-For-Sport-And-Physical-Exercise-,-a-,-Activity (accessed 27 May 2021).

603. SportSG (11 Jun 2021), *Calibrated Easing of Safe Management Measures for Sport and Physical Exercise & Activity from 14 June 2021*, https://www.sportsingapore.gov.sg/-/media/SSC/Corporate/Files/News-and-Updates/Media-Releases/2021/June/14/Final---Calibrated-Easing-of-SMM-for-Sport_PE_PA-(11-Jun-21).pdf?la=en&hash=7E082F621F642957714FB6B09AD5BDE4B09A86EB (accessed 15 Jun. 2021).

604. ActiveSG (20 Feb. 2021), *Singapore Tennis Open 2021 – All You Need to Know*, https://circle.myactivesg.com/circle-news/articles/singapore-tennis-open-2021-all-you-need-to-know (accessed 3 May 2021).

605. Mr Edwin Tong Chun Fai (8 Mar. 2021), *Singapore Parliamentary Report*, vol. 95, sitting no. 27, https://sprs.parl.gov.sg/search/#/sprs3topic?reportid=budget-1638 (accessed 3 May 2021).

606. Ministry of Health (23 Jan. 2020), *Confirmed Imported Case Of Novel Coronavirus Infection in Singapore; Multi-Ministry Taskforce Ramps Up Precautionary Measures*, https://www.moh.gov.sg/news-highlights/details/confirmed-imported-case-of-novel-coronavirus-infection-in-singapore-multi-ministry-taskforce-ramps-up-precautionary-measures (accessed 3 May 2021).

cushion the blow that the pandemic has had on individuals, households and businesses. With regard to sports, the Minister for Culture, Community and Youth announced the roll-out of the SGD 50 million Sports Resilience Package on 15 October 2020.[607] SportSG released further details on 19 November 2020.[608] On 8 March 2021, the Minister announced that an additional SGD 25 million would be provided to enhance the package.[609] Some details of the package, as at June 2021, are set out below.

534. For businesses, the Operating Grant provides support for entities, including private academies and clubs, private league operators and facility operators, which contribute to athlete pipeline development. Eligible entities receive an equivalent of about 25% of their total operating expenses, capped at SGD 15,000 per month for up to six months, until December 2021. As at 8 March 2021, close to one hundred businesses had benefited from the Operating Grant.[610]

535. The Blended Initiative Grant supports event management companies, event organisers and private academies and clubs in the development of event and programme innovation that engage participants in 'phygital' event formats and/or programmes.

536. The Enterprise Innovation and Capability Development Grant seeks to support the development and application of technology and/or innovative solutions in the sports industry, by helping sport and fitness enterprises in developing and/or applying solutions to take their business to the next level, and enterprises in adjacent industries (e.g., technology) to develop solutions for the sports industry. Projects supported should cover at least one of various categories, including fan or consumer engagement, high performance and sports science, next-generation infrastructure and facilities, or health and wellness.

537. Coaches registered under the NROC can apply for the Continuing Coach Education Training Allowance, and the Structured Mentoring Programme. The former allows the coach to claim for continuing coaching education courses, up to a maximum of thirty hours. The latter provides a monthly allowance. The support will be provided until March 2022.

538. Sports self-employed persons are eligible for the SEP Project Grant. This grant supports sports self-employed persons to collaborate with one another and

---

607. Mr Edwin Tong Chun Fai (15 Oct. 2020), *Singapore Parliamentary Report*, vol. 95, sitting no. 10, https://sprs.parl.gov.sg/search/#/sprs3topic?reportid=ministerial-statement-1512 (accessed 3 May 2021).
608. SportSG (17 Nov. 2020), *Sports Resilience Package to Boost Industry Capabilities and Help Businesses Stay Ahead of the Curve*, https://www.sportsingapore.gov.sg/Newsroom/Media-Releases/2020/Sports-Resilience-Package-to-boost-industry-capabilities-and-help-businesses-stay-ahead-of-the-curve (accessed 3 May 2021).
609. Mr Edwin Tong Chun Fai (8 Mar. 2021), *Singapore Parliamentary Report*, vol. 95, sitting no. 27, https://sprs.parl.gov.sg/search/#/sprs3topic?reportid=budget-1638 (accessed 3 May 2021).
610. *Ibid.*

other organisations to develop projects that enhance the health and wellness of Singaporeans. The grant for each application is capped at SGD 25,000 or up to 70% of qualifying costs, which are specifically operating costs for running projects, events or programmes. Project teams must comprise at least one self-employed person registered with organisations, such as the NROC. As at May 2021, close to forty projects comprising individual or group participants have been awarded with about SGD 315,000.[611]

539. Separately, sports self-employed persons who have experienced an income loss of at least 50% for at least one month during the period from 8 May 2021 to 30 June 2021 may apply for the COVID-19 Recovery Grant (Temporary) scheme. Eligible individuals may receive a one-off payout of up to SGD 500.[612]

540. For businesses and individuals, the Digital Content Development Grant seeks to help self-employed professionals, freelance coaches and businesses enhance the quality of digital sport productions and expand their reach by hosting the content on a virtual platform. Successful applicants receive between SGD 80,000 and SGD 150,000 to produce content that must be directly or indirectly sport related that will encourage the target audience in learning new skills, being inspired and/or increasing participation.

541. Outside of the Sports Resilience Package, SportSG also created more than nine hundred temporary jobs for sports sector professionals whose livelihoods have been affected.[613] The Government has also set up a number of financial assistance schemes that can apply to sports. For example, the Jobs Support Scheme provides wage support to employers to retain local employees. An employer (such as a football team) can receive a cash grant of 10% to 75% of the first SGD 4,600 of gross monthly wages paid to each employee between October 2019 and September 2021.[614] For coaches and self-employed persons, the Temporary Relief Fund provided a one-off payment of SGD 500 for the month of April 2020 to those who had lost their job or at least 30% of personal income due to COVID-19, subject to qualifying income criteria of not more than the monthly income of SGD 3,100 or gross monthly household income of SGD 10,000. The COVID-19 Recovery Grant provides up to SGD 700 per month, for those months, for those who had lost employment or salary loss of at least 50%.[615]

---

611. SportSG (28 May 2021), *SportSG Updates Sport Resilience Package for businesses and SEPs*, https://www.sportsingapore.gov.sg/Newsroom/Media-Releases/2021/May/SportSG-updates-Sport-Resilience-Package-for-businesses-and-SEPs, para. 11 (accessed 15 Jun. 2021).
612. *Ibid.*, para. 5.
613. Ministry for Culture, Community and Youth (22 Jun. 2020), *MCCY Unveils Plans for Sport Sector in Singapore*, https://www.mccy.gov.sg/about-us/news-and-resources/press-statements/2020/jun/mccy-unveils-plans-for-sport-sector-in-singapore, para. 10 (accessed 3 May 2021).
614. Inland Revenue Authority of Singapore, *Jobs Support Scheme (JSS)*, https://www.iras.gov.sg/irashome/schemes/businesses/jobs-support-scheme--JSS-/ (accessed 3 May 2021).
615. Ministry of Social and Family Development, *COVID-19 Recovery Grant*, https://www.msf.gov.sg/assistance/Pages/covid-recovery-grant.aspx (accessed 3 May 2021).

542. In March 2022, a campaign titled 'Bring Sport Back' was announced. Its purpose was to ramp up and cater to the increasing post-COVID demand for sport.[616] The campaign aimed to facilitate the reintroduction of mass participation in sports events, ramp up community participation in sports through more group activities, and optimise sports facilities. The campaign included grants of up to SGD 50,000 to fund mass participation in sports events.

616. Mr Edwin Tong Chun Fai (10 Mar. 2022), *Singapore Parliamentary Report,* vol. 95, sitting no. 58, available at https://sprs.parl.gov.sg/search/#/sprs3topic?reportid=budget-1898 (accessed 29 Nov. 2023).

Conclusion

543. In the authors' opinion, Singapore does not currently have a distinct body of legal principles and doctrine that can be defined as 'sports law'. There is no sports-specific legislation (other than the administrative legislation that governs SportSG).

544. NSAs have a certain level of autonomy in rule-making and enforcing, hence if there is a dispute that can be dealt with internally by an NSA (e.g., a dispute between athletes or between the athlete and the NSA), then the NSA may do so. The existence of the dispute and how the dispute is resolved are not necessarily reported.

545. If there is a potentially criminal act, then intervention by the authorities is more likely, and the matter would then be dealt with through exercise of relevant and appropriate statutory provisions (e.g., the Penal Code or the MDAct).

546. Other sports-related issues may be dealt with under other legislation, such as legislation relating to intellectual property law, contract law, employment law and media law. The common law also plays a part, especially with regard to tortious claims (e.g., for negligence, defamation, passing off or harassment).

547. The Government of Singapore has been in recent years increasing efforts to promote sports for all, to focus on sports excellence and to provide more funding for sports. These developments in the sports industry may eventually lead to a corresponding increase and development of sports-related common law and sports-specific legislation.

Selected Bibliography

Print Sources

Gary Chan, Kok Yew. *The Law of Torts in Singapore.* 2nd ed., Academy Publishing, 2016.

Michael, A. Jones, Anthony M Dugdale & Mark Simpson, *Clerk and Lindsell on Torts.* 21st ed., Sweet and Maxwell, 2014.

Sentencing Practice in the Subordinate Courts. vol. II, 3rd ed., LexisNexis, 2013.

Singapore Sports Guide 2013/2014. 8th ed., Marshall Cavendish, 2013.

Singapore Sports Guide 2015/2016. 10th ed., Marshall Cavendish, 2015.

Tan, David. *The Celebrity Halo Effect and Passing Off.* Singapore Law Gazette, LexisNexis, July 2017.

Web Sources

Webpages within the following parent websites:

Active Citizens Worldwide: https://web.archive.org/web/20220123143330/https://activecitizens.world/.

ActiveSG: https://www.myactivesg.com and https://circle.myactivesg.com/.

Adweek: https://www.adweek.com/.

AsiaOne: http://www.asiaone.com/.

BBC News: https://www.bbc.com/.

Berita Harian: https://www.beritaharian.sg/.

Blogpage operated by Mr Lee Kin Mun: https://www.mrbrown.com/.

Bouygues Construction: https://www.bouygues-construction.com/.

Brands Singapore: https://www.brandsworld.com.sg/.

Central Manpower Base: https://www.cmpb.gov.sg/web/portal/cmpb/home/.

Channel NewsAsia: https://www.channelnewsasia.com/.

Commissioner of Charities: https://www.charities.gov.sg/.

Eurosport Asia: https://asia.eurosport.com/.

Fitness First Singapore: https://www.fitnessfirst.com.sg/.

Football Association of Singapore: http://www.fas.org.sg/.

Global Lottery Monitoring System: http://glms-sport.org/.

Goal: http://www.goal.com/.

Government of Singapore: https://www.gov.sg/.

IEG: http://www.sponsorship.com/.

Infocomm Media Authority: https://www.imda.gov.sg/.

Inland Revenue of Singapore: https://www.iras.gov.sg/.

Selected Bibliography

MediaCorp: https://www.MediaCorp.sg/.
Ministry of Culture, Community and Youth: https://www.mccy.gov.sg/.
Ministry of Defence: https://www.mindef.gov.sg/web/portal/mindef/home.
Ministry of Health: https://www.moh.gov.sg/.
Ministry of Home Affairs: https://www.mha.gov.sg/.
National Archives of Singapore: http://www.nas.gov.sg/.
OCBC Group: https://www.ocbc.com/group/group-home.html.
Premier League: https://www.premierleague.com/.
Safe Sport International: https://www.safesportinternational.com/.
Singapore Badminton Association: http://www.singaporebadminton.org.sg/.
Singapore Chess Federation: https://www.singaporechess.org.sg/.
Singapore Golf Association: https://www.sga.org.sg.
Singapore Hockey Federation: http://www.singaporehockey.org/.
Singapore Ice Skating Association: https://www.sisa.org.sg.
Singapore National Olympic Council: http://www.singaporeolympics.com/.
Singapore Parliamentary Reports: https://sprs.parl.gov.sg/search/#/home.
Singapore Police Force: https://www.police.gov.sg/.
Singapore Sailing Federation: https://sailing.org.sg.
Singapore Shooting Association: https://singaporeshooting.org/portal/.
Singapore Sports School: https://www.sportsschool.edu.sg/.
Singapore Swimming Association: http://www.swimming.org.sg/.
Singapore Table Tennis Association: http://www.stta.org.sg/.
Singtel: https://www.singtel.com/.
Southeast Asia Regional Anti-Doping Organization: https://www.searado.com/.
Sport Singapore: https://www.sportsingapore.gov.sg/.
The Guardian: https://www.theguardian.com/.
The New Paper: https://www.tnp.sg.
The South China Morning Post: https://www.scmp.com/.
The Straits Times: https://www.straitstimes.com/.
Today: https://www.todayonline.com/.
Transparency Market Research: https://www.transparencymarketresearch.com/.
World Anti-Doping Agency: https://www.wada-ama.org/.
World Health Organization: https://www.who.int/.

Index

The numbers here refer to paragraph numbers.

Index